Volume 2

Advances in
Doctoral Research
in Management

Volume 2

Advances in
Doctoral Research
in Management

Editor Luiz Moutinho
University of Glasgow, UK

Associate Editor Kun-Huang Huarng
Feng Chia University, Taiwan

 **World Scientific**

NEW JERSEY · LONDON · SINGAPORE · BEIJING · SHANGHAI · HONG KONG · TAIPEI · CHENNAI

Published by

World Scientific Publishing Co. Pte. Ltd.

5 Toh Tuck Link, Singapore 596224

USA office: 27 Warren Street, Suite 401-402, Hackensack, NJ 07601

UK office: 57 Shelton Street, Covent Garden, London WC2H 9HE

British Library Cataloguing-in-Publication Data
A catalogue record for this book is available from the British Library.

Advances in Doctoral Research in Management – Vol. 2
ADVANCES IN DOCTORAL RESEARCH IN MANAGEMENT
Copyright © 2008 by World Scientific Publishing Co. Pte. Ltd.

ISBN-13 978-981-277-865-9
ISBN-10 981-277-865-9

Typeset by Stallion Press
Email: enquiries@stallionpress.com

Printed in Singapore.

To all the doctoral students who show excellence in research.
Luiz

To my wife Tiffany, and my children Andy and
David for your love and support.
Kun-Huang

Advances in Doctoral Research in Management (ADRM) is a refereed academic research book series which publishes an annual volume devoted to disseminate excellence in doctoral research in management. It publishes seminal and challenging international doctoral research that could be seen as a benchmark in academic effectiveness which embraces the whole spectrum of academic research philosophies (from phenomenological/ideographic to positivistic/nomothetic research).

Aims and Scope

- To provide a robust refereed outlet for doctoral researchers in the management/business field.
- To encourage doctoral candidates to disseminate their work and receive positive and constructive feedback on their research projects.
- To create a "focused forum and stage" in which some of the new and (potentially important) future research paradigms will be presented and tested among academics.
- To become a most relevant academic publication in terms of the introduction of methodological issues, techniques and approaches which will ultimately benefit doctoral students, their supervisors and other researchers.

The planned scope will entail the following perspectives:

- The annual volume's coverage is cross-disciplinary since it entails all doctoral research output in the broad areas of management and business.
- The main management disciplines from which it is expected to derive submissions will include marketing, strategy, international business, operations management, organisational behaviour, human resource management, organisational systems, finance, managerial economics and technology management.

CONTENTS

DOCTORAL RESEARCH NOTES   103

RESEARCH METHODOLOGY PAPERS   149

ACKNOWLEDGMENTS

We would like to thank:

The editorial board members, and Hooi-Yean Lee, Cheong Chean Chian, Yvonne Tan Hui Ling, and Teng Poh Hoon of World Scientific Publishing for their help with the publication of this volume.

ABOUT THE EDITORS

Luiz Moutinho

Professor of Marketing, University of Glasgow. He completed his PhD at the University of Sheffield in 1982 and held posts at Cardiff Business School, University of Wales College of Cardiff, Cleveland State University, Ohio, USA, Northern Arizona University, USA and California State University, USA, as well as visiting Professorship positions in New Zealand and Brazil. Between 1987 and 1989 he was the Director of the Doctoral Programmes at the Confederation of Scottish Business Schools and at the Cardiff Business School between 1993 and 1996. He was Director of the Doctoral Programme at the University of Glasgow, School of Business and Management between 1996 and 2004. He is the Editor of the Advances in Doctoral Research in Management (ADRM), and the Journal of Modelling in Management.

One of Professor Moutinho's primary areas of academic research is related to modelling processes of consumer behaviour. He has developed a number of conceptual models over the years in areas such as tourism destination decision processes, automated banking, supermarket patronage, among other areas. The testing of these research models has been based on the application of many different statistical computer modelling techniques ranging from multidimensional scaling, multinomial logit and linear structural relations to neural networks, ordered probit and tabu search.

He has published 19 books:

Problems in Marketing — Analysis and Applications (2004), second edition, co-authored (lead author) with Charles S Chien. Published by SAGE.
Strategic Marketing (2003), co-authored with Laszlo Jozsa (Elsevier)
Strategic Management in Tourism (2000). Published by CABI.

Contemporary Issues in Marketing, co-authored with Martin Evans (MacMillan Business 1999)

Strategic Planning Systems in Hospitality and Tourism, co-authored with Paul Phillips (CABI 1998).

Quantitative Analysis in Marketing Management, co-authored with Mark Goode and Fiona Davies (Wiley 1998).

Financial Services Marketing — A Reader, co-edited with Arthur Meidan and Barbara Lewis (The Dryden Press 1997).

Applied Consumer Behaviour (1996), co-authored with Martin Evans and Fred van Raaif. Published by Addison-Wesley.

Expert Systems in Tourism Marketing (1996), co-authored (lead author) with Paulo Rita and Bruce Curry. Published by the International Thomson Business Press.

Tourist Marketing and Management Handbook (1995), Student Edition, co-edited with Stephen F Witt. Published by Prentice-Hall International.

Cases in Marketing Management (1995), second edition. Published by Addison-Wesley.

Computer Modelling and Expert Systems in Marketing (1994), co-authored (lead author) with Bruce Curry, Fiona Davies and Paulo Rita. Published by Routledge.

Tourism Marketing and Management Handbook (1994), second edition, co-edited with Stephen F. Witt. Published by Prentice-Hall International.

Cases in Marketing of Services — An International Collection (1993), co-edited with Arthur Meidan. Published by Addison-Wesley.

Applied Marketing Research (1992), co-authored (lead author) with Martin Evans. Published by Addison-Wesley.

Problems in Marketing: Analysis and Applications (1991). Published by Paul Chapman Publishing.

Managing and Marketing Services in the 1990's (1990), co-edited with Richard Teare and Neil Morgan. Published by Cassell plc, England.

Cases in Marketing Management (1989). Published by Addison-Wesley.

Tourism Marketing and Management Handbook (1989), co-edited with Stephen F. Witt. Published by Prentice-Hall International.

He has over 350 refereed international publications.

In addition to presenting papers at many international conferences, he also has had a vast number of articles published in journals such as

Journal of Business Research, Journal of Marketing Management, European Journal of Marketing, Journal of Strategic Marketing, Service Industries Journal, Journal of EuroMarketing, Journal of International Consumer Marketing, International Journal of Advertising, International Journal of Bank Marketing, Journal of General Management, European Management Journal, Journal of Professional Services Marketing, International Journal of Retail and Distribution Management, Irish Marketing Review, Journal of Marketing Channels, International Journal of Service Industry Management, Quarterly Review of Marketing, Marketing Intelligence and Planning, Journal of Retailing and Consumer Services among others. He is also a member of the Editorial Board of several international academic journals. Professor Moutinho has also received a number of awards for excellence in academic research in the USA, UK and Portugal.

Luiz Moutinho has been a full Professor of Marketing since 1989 and was appointed in 1996 to the Foundation Chair of Marketing at the University of Glasgow. He holds Visiting Professorships at the University of Vilnius, Lithuania, Bled School of Management, Slovenia and Feng Chia University, Taiwan. Has run teaching courses and research seminars in Denmark, France, Holland, USA, Brazil, Mexico, Spain, Portugal, Italy, Croatia, Slovenia, Hungary, Greece, Lithuania, Finland, Taiwan, Australia, New Zealand, Austria, Mozambique and Mongolia.

Kun-Huang Huarng

Kun-Huang Huarng received the B.S. degree in electronic engineering from Chung Yuan Christian University, Taiwan, in 1984, and the M.S. and Ph.D. degrees in computer science from Texas A&M University, College Station, USA, in 1989 and 1993, respectively. He was with the Department of Finance, Chaoyang University of Technology, Taiwan, from 1995 to 2001, where he also worked as the Director of Library from 1996 to 2000. Since 2001, he has been with the Department of International Trade, Feng Chia University, Taiwan, where he has been a Professor since 2002; worked as Associate Dean, the College of Business and the Director of Electronic Commerce Research Institute. He is currently the Head Librarian. His current research interests include computer modeling and e-commerce. Professor Huarng is a member of Upsilon Pi Epsilon; Editor of Journal of Economics and Management; Associate Editor of Journal of Modelling in Management; Associate Editor, Advances in Doctoral Research in Management; Associate Editor of International Journal of Culture, Tourism and Hospitality

Research; Guest Editor of Portuguese Journal of Management Studies. He was listed in Marquis Who's Who in the World in 1996.

Selected publications

Yu, Tiffany. H.-K. and Huarng, K.-H., "A Bivariate Fuzzy Time Series Model to Forecast the TAIEX," Expert Systems with Applications, 36(3), December 2008.

Huarng, K., Yu, Tiffany H.-K. and Hsu, Yu Wei, "A Multivariate Heuristic Model for Fuzzy Time Series Forecasting," *IEEE Transactions on Systems, Man and Cybernetics Part B*, 37(4), August 2007, 836–846.

Huarng, K., Moutinho, Yu, L. and Tiffany H.-K., "An Advanced Approach to Forecasting Tourism Demand in Taiwan," *Journal of Travel and Tourism Marketing*, special issue on New Quantitative Models in Travel and Tourism Research, 21(4), June 12, 2007.

Huarng, K. and Yu, Tiffany H.-K., "The Application of Neural Networks to Forecast Fuzzy Time Series," *Physica A*, 363(2), May 2006, pp. 481–491.

Huarng, K. and Yu, Tiffany H.-K., "Ratio-based Lengths of Intervals to Improve Fuzzy Time Series Forecasting," *IEEE Transactions on Systems, Man and Cybernetics Part B*, 36(2), April 2006, pp. 328–340.

Huarng, K. and Yu, H.-K., "A type 2 fuzzy time series model for stock index forecasting," *Physica A*, 353, August 2005, pp. 445–462.

Huarng, K., "Heuristic Models of Fuzzy Times Series for Forecasting," *Fuzzy Sets and Systems*, 123(3), 2001, pp. 369–386.

Huarng, K., "Effective Lengths of Intervals to Improve Forecasting in Fuzzy Times Series," *Fuzzy Sets and Systems*, 123(3), 2001, pp. 387–394.

Ching, H.S. and Huarng, K., "Using the Internet as a Catalyst for Asia-Pacific Regional Economic Cooperation: An Example of New Chinese Networks," *Technology in Society*, 20(2), 1998, pp. 131–139.

Huarng, K., "Heuristic Resolution for Multiple Inheritance in Object-Oriented Expert System Building Tools," *Information Sciences: An International Journal*, 98(1–4), 1997, pp. 43–67.

Huarng, K. and Simmons, D.B., "An Object Knowledge Canonical Form for Knowledge Reuse," *Expert Systems with Applications: An International Journal*, 10(1), 1996/1, pp. 135–146.

LIST OF CONTRIBUTORS

Dr Kathleen Riach
School of Accounting, Finance and Management
University of Essex
Wivenhoe Park
Colchester CO4 3SQ
kriach@essex.ac.uk

Professor Fiona Wilson
Department of Management
Gilbert Scott Building
University of Glasgow
Glasgow, UK, G12 8QQ
F.Wilson@mgt.gla.ac.uk

Konstantinos Tolikas
Cardiff Business School
Cardiff University
Aberconway Building
Colum Drive
Cardiff, CF10 3EU, UK
Tel: +44 2920 876652
Fax: +44 2920 874419
Email: TolikasK@cardiff.ac.uk

Anthony C. Antonakis
Department of Business Administration
University of Piraeus
Greece

Michael E. Sfakianakis
Department of Business Administration
University of Piraeus
Greece

Shu-Meei Ho
Department of International Trade
Chihlee Institute of Technology
Email: shuho@mail.chihlee.edu.tw

Berlin Wu
Department of Mathematical Sciences
National ChengChi University, Taiwan
Email: Berlin@nccu.edu.tw

Dr Xuemei Bian
Room 219, Esk Building
Business School
University of Hull
Cottingham Road
Hull, HU6 7RX
Tel: 0044 1482 464547
Fax: 0044 1482 463623
Email: x.bian@hull.ac.uk

Fernando Augusto de Sá Neves dos Santos
Management Department
Escola Superior de Tecnologia e Gestão of
    Instituto Politécnico da Guarda
Portugal
Email: fneves@ipg.pt

Elizabeth Reis
Department of Quantitative Methods
ISCTE Business School
Lisbon, Portugal
Email: ear@iscte.pt

Sören Lüeders
Avenida de los Naranjos
s/n, Facultad d'Economia
University of Valencia
Valencia, 46022, Spain

Luisa Andreu
Avenida de los Naranjos
s/n, Facultad d'Economia
University of Valencia
Valencia, 46022, Spain

Anna S. Mattila
224 Mateer Building
University Park
School of Hospitality Management
Pennsylvania State University
Pennsylvania, PA 16802-1307, United States
Email: asm6@psu.edu

E. Pavlidis
Department of Economics
University of Lancaster Management School

I. Paya
Department of Economics
University of Lancaster Management School

D. A. Peel
Department of Economics
University of Lancaster Management School

Junzo Watada
Graduate School of Information, Production and Systems
Waseda University
2-7 Hibikino, Wakamatsu
Kitakyushu 808-0135, Japan
watada@waseda.jp

EDITORIAL

We are pleased to introduce the second volume of Advances in Doctoral Research in Management (ADRM). This book series has been designed to fill an academic dissertation gap with regard to excellence in doctoral research in management. Although its format looks like a research book, its content and reviewing process functions like a robust academic journal. This second volume contains a wide variety of topics, structured as competitive papers, research notes, and methodology papers, ranging from organisational romance, extreme value theory, Naïve Bayes scorecards, industrial networks, and counterfeit products to materialism in Europe, convertible debt issuance, pricing/customer relationship, bootstrapping, and DNA computing.

Despite organisational romance being heralded as an important managerial issue 30 years ago, there remains a lack of academic research exploring nonplatonic workplace relationship. In light of this discrepancy, Riach and Wilson seek to move organisational romance away from the managerialist rhetoric which adopts a rationalist, prescriptive approach, and towards the sexuality and organisation literature. Workplace romance can be thus viewed as an integral workplace dynamic, imbued with issues of power and politics at both a macro- and a local-level. To explore how this may be played out in practice, data from interviews was subjected to a number of narrative analysis techniques to demonstrate how organisational romance is discussed, negotiate, and played out in a workplace.

Tolikas applies extreme value theory (EVT) methods to investigate the asymptotic distributions of the extreme minima and maxima of the Athens Stock Exchange daily returns over the period 1976–2001. New aspects are covered in this paper, including (1) the generalised extreme value and generalised logistic distributions are considered, (2) L-moments ratio diagrams are used to identify the distributions most likely to fit the extreme daily returns, (3) the probability weighted moments is used to estimate the parameters of the distributions, and (4) the Anderson–Darling goodness of fit test is employed to test the adequacy of fit. As a result, the generalised logistic distribution is found to provide adequate descriptions of the behavior of both the extreme minima and maxima over the period studied.

Antonakis and Sfakianakis examine the effectiveness of the Naïve Bayes Rule in constructing scorecards to discriminate the credit applicants. The performance of the constructed scorecard is evaluated by a real-world data sample. Unfortunately, Naïve Bayes is found to produce the worst-performing scorecard under both measures used.

In the traditional market research methods, most questionnaires' design is set up with a binary logic. Ho and Wu consider that people often encounter uncertainty or imprecision problems when they fill the survey. To develop a more efficient survey analysis, they propose the methods for applying fuzzy mode, fuzzy expect value, and the fuzzy test. By the methods, a new design of market survey process and analysis is proposed and a comparison between the fuzzy test and the traditional test is conducted.

Bian examines the determinants of likelihood of consideration of counterfeit branded luxury handbags in the context of nondeceptive counterfeiting. The effects of consumer-perceived brand personality, benefits, product attributes, perceived risks, and consumer demographic variables are anticipated and explored. Focus groups are used to generate criteria which consumers used to evaluate studied brands, and a survey research is used to collect data for the main study. Generalised linear modeling (GLM) analyses reveal that the brand personality is the dominant factor in determining the likelihood of the consideration of the counterfeit branded luxury products. In general, the perceived risks and the demographic variables do not appear to be significantly influential on the formation of the consideration set in the context of nondeceptive counterfeiting.

The main objective of the chapter by Santos and Reis is to examine the invariance of Richins and Dawson's (1992) previously validated three-factor materialism model scale across different cultural groups of respondents and to analyse and estimate the presence of materialistic values among Europeans, more precisely in the samples from Germany, Spain, and Portugal. Through Richins and Dawson's (1992) materialism values scale, they have checked and cross-examined the materialistic dimensions among the young people of the countries referred to using structural equation modelling (SEM). They have found that there are different levels and sorts of materialism between the three European countries.

Yang and Xia investigate the effect of issuing convertible debt in product market competition. When there is Cournot quantity competition, under the assumption of no default risk and normal random returns, they consider that the issuance of convertible debt may impose a negative effect on the outcome equilibrium for the issuing firm. Hence, the contingent feature of convertible debt can serve as a committing device for a more conservative attitude for the issuing firm, and thus may stimulate the competitors' aggressive strategy. This strategic disadvantage explains the long-run underperformance of convertible debt after issuance.

Lüders *et al.* develop a pricing framework that focuses on relationship-building — a factor that has been largely ignored in the pricing literature. They first employ a case-study method to better understand how a production-oriented company sets prices for its products. Then, they have developed a framework that incorporates the service component in the pricing equation. The results of this research suggest that factoring in the price for services offered can enhance relationship management, thus having a positive impact on the company's business performance. Misspecification of a true model, which does not exhibit non-normal or heteroskedastic errors, could result in non-normal or heteroskedasticity errors in the estimated, and incorrect, functional form.

So how can we make appropriate statistical inferences? Pavlidis *et al.* discuss two methods. Both exploit recent advances in computing. The first of these is known as the wild bootstrap. The method can be employed when the sample size is small. This method is appropriate when the error term in a regression exhibits heteroskedasticity and the error is either normally or non-normally distributed. Under such conditions the wild bootstrap has been shown to be an appropriate method for determining appropriate critical values for t- and F-tests. The second method is only appropriate when the error term exhibits non-normality. The method involves simulating errors from the generalised lambda distribution. The intuition behind both the wild bootstrap approach and the generalised lambda approach is to identify the distributions of relevant test statistic when the null hypothesis holds and the distribution of regression residuals is based on the relevant sample distribution.

Watada illustrates the method of DNA computing. In the problem of group control of elevators, we may face problems such that all elevators are moving in the same direction or that all elevators arrive at the same floor. To resolve such problems, all elevators should be controlled properly. DNA computing is shown to calculate the complex problems of a group of elevators and a huge number of floors. The optimal solution is then presented.

We hope that you enjoy reading this diversity of ontological and epistemological views as well as the myriad of research methodology approaches and methods (technologies) utilised. Above all, we really hope that these scholarly pieces of work would benefit you in your doctoral research studies.

Glasgow, Scotland
1 July, 2007

Luiz Moutinho
Kun-Huang Huarng

DOCTORAL RESEARCH PAPERS

1

ORGANISATIONAL ROMANCE: THEORISING AND RESEARCHING AN UNDEREXPLORED PHENOMENON

Kathleen Riach*

University of Essex, UK

Fiona Wilson

University of Glasgow, UK

Despite organisational romance being heralded as an important managerial issue 30 years ago by Quinn (1977) there remains a lack of academic research exploring non-platonic workplace relationships. In light of this discrepancy, this chapter seeks to move organisational romance away from the managerialist rhetoric which adopts a rationalist, prescriptive approach, and towards the sexuality and organisation literature. Workplace romance can be thus viewed as an integral workplace dynamic, imbued with issues of power and politics at both a macro and local level. To explore how this may be played out in practice, data from 48 interviews were subjected to a number of narrative analysis techniques to demonstrate how organisational romance is discussed, negotiated, and played out in a workplace.

Keywords: Organisational romance; work; romance; sexuality; rules.

1. Introduction

As early as 1974, Donald Roy (1974, p. 44) noted that "sex is a commonly overlooked aspect of informal social organisation". Moreover, his chapter, published in a book entitled *Deviant Behaviour*, gives us an insight into how

---

*Corresponding author.

sexual relations at work were assumed to be an unwarranted and illegitimate aspect of the bureaucratic organisation. Yet, 4 decades of academic writing appears to have done little to challenge this conception. While the media feed on a public desire for work-sex scandals, such as President Clinton's extra-curricular activities with his subordinates (see Powell, 2000), the managerial literature has remained sceptical about the legitimacy of conducting affairs at work. However, there remains a lack of empirically informed research about the incidence, perceptions, and consequences of workplace romance, with many reports being informed through colloquial accounts or stereo-typical reproductions of gender roles. To provide a means of enlightening current debates on this organisational phenomenon, this chapter sets out to critical overview the existing literature and situate workplace romances within the theoretical commitments posited within a "sexuality of organisa-tion" perspective, before empirically investigating managers and employers perceptions and experiences of organisational romance.

2. Research Traditions in Organisational Romance

Within the body of mainly North-American scholarly literature, workplace romances are defined as mutually desired relationships between two people at work, in which some element of sexuality or physical intimacy exists (Powell and Foley, 1998). Romances at work have long been occurring, understood mainly through psychological theories of likeability, which states we are attracted to those similar to us or who work in the same corporate culture or occupation (Maniero, 1986; Smith et al., 1993). The rise in number of such relationships has also been credited to a range of social and cultural changes in both work and private spheres. Developed countries have all undergone sociodemographic changes, such as later ages for marriage, higher divorce rates, and a higher proportion of unmarried people, all of which creates a greater potential courtship pool at work (Hearn and Parkin, 1987). Trends in working have also seen individuals work longer hours and ascribe to cultural norms which facilitate socialising outside the workplace (Pierce et al., 1996).

One central research theme has been exploring perceptions of those who are around the couple, rather than those participating in the romance them-selves, implying that the relationship will have an inevitable affect on the immediate work group. Using survey methods, studies have demonstrated that non-hierarchical relationships, reported to be the most common form of relationship (Alfred Marks Bureau, 1991; Girvin, 1995) are seen as accept-able with little need for managerial intervention (Training and Development Journal, 1994; Fisher, 1994). Warfield (1987) even suggests that there may be positive outcomes, such as enhancing work environments. Hierarchical work relationships are viewed as more detrimental, raising issues of career rewards, such as promotion or job assignments being given unfairly (Greenberg, 1987) and skewing the bureaucratic chain of authority and command.

However, regardless of an inter or intra-hierarchical relationship, research has provided a caveat that the romance should not interfere with the day-to-day running of the business. With the current literature following a Weberian logic of bureaucracy where organisations are viewed as operating "without regard for persons" (Weber, 1948, p. 975), the highly emotive characteristic that defines romance is ultimately at a disjuncture with ideologies of how the workplace operates. It is thus unsurprising that the literature is heavily slanted towards managerialist rhetoric and serves to accentuate the negative consequences of romance at work, such as the possibility of legal action should attraction become one-sided once the romance is terminated (Pierce and Aguinis, 1997; Pierce *et al.*, 2000). Indeed, scare-figures have been used as a reason to sanction romance altogether: one survey for the Society for Human Resource Management (1998) predicted (but did not prove) that 24% of romances would end in sexual harassment claims (Wilson *et al.*, 2003).

What is not challenged within current literature is that the "disruption" caused is highly subjective and often cannot be directly attributable to the romance itself. Indeed, it may lead to the romance being used as an excuse for derision of the colleagues, rather than a legitimate complaint. Other issues of political manoeuvring and power have also been negated within current studies, although there are clear signs of disparities between perceived gender roles. Some research has tentatively suggested that women are more at risk of negative evaluations following a romance (Quinn, 1977; Maniero, 1993), underlined in surveys where the stereotype of a women "sleeping her way to the top" or participating in the relationship for motives other than romance is clearly signalled (Powell, 2000; Anderson and Hunsaker, 1985). This is neither challenged or reproached by the articles, with many attributing the rise in workplace romance to an increase of women in the labour force which is seen to upset "traditional organisational behaviour modes" (Warfield, 1987, p. 22) and cause numerous "problems" for personnel departments (Ford and Mclaughlin, 1987). In doing so, many articles are in danger of blaming women for workplace romance, rather than exploring how inequities occur.

As suggested, this body of literature has yet to explore the full complexity of workplace romance, both in terms of the gendered power relations, and providing a well-rounded, critical assessment of its impact. With many of the studies published within popularist of manager-focused journals, organisational romance is rationalised as something that can be understood, managed, and effectively "solved" through traditional techniques or 5-point plans (see Schaefer and Tudor, 2001). The danger of not challenging organisational romance is presented in a heavily biased manner by often focusing on the potentially apocalyptic and "destructive" consequences (Warfield, 1987, p. 22), not only for employee relations, but for the very basis of the organisational structures (Collins, 1983). The scope and definition of organisational romance also remains underdeveloped through the limited methodological approaches, where surveys or vignettes concentrate on third-party perceptions of heterosexual relationships, failing to question the experiences of those involved in a relationship themselves (e.g., Harrison and Lee, 1985; Karl and Sutton, 2000). Indeed, it appears that to develop a better understanding of this phenomenon, there is a need to problematise how we identify and theoretically conceptualise workplace romance.

3. "Sexualising" Organisational Romance

In response to a managerial rationalistic bias within studies of human activities in the workplace, organisational behaviour has witnessed a transition towards more postmodernist and critical-influenced approaches to the theory of work which seek to disrupt the norms and assumptions that are accepted as constituting organisational life (Alvesson, 2002). Instead of placing value on what can be seen, proven, and factualised, critical theory has sought to develop a way of breaking down the taken-for-granted and instead focuses upon the processes through which organisational artefact and identities are socially constructed in relation to power and politics.

Within this terrain, sexuality has been called the "most taboo topics within contemporary organisation theory" (Hancock and Tyler, 2001, p. 150), inevitably silenced to the detriment of its study as a workplace phenomenon (Brewis and Linstead, 2000). Yet sexuality in organisations continued to exist and can be seen as mutually constructed by each other (Hearn and Parkin, 1987). Gendered identities have been strongly associated with ways of managing, where the masculine is aligned with assertive, aggressive traits, leaving females to be marginalised by deviating from a male norm, in accentuated gender positions characterised by being overemotional and the need to support, rather than lead (Trethewey, 1999). Likewise, sexuality may be interpreted as embodied, literally "written upon" the gestures, clothes, and appearance of women and men at work. Although these may come to stand for an aesthetic form of economy where specific cultural values of the organisation are inscribed on or through the body (Tyler and Abbot, 1998; Entwistle, 2002), it is inevitable that sexuality plays a role in the way we make meaning or send out messages about what the organisation stands for and, in turn how we come to understand our own and others' employee identity.

If sexuality is embedded within organisational life, it is inevitable that explicit activities relating to sexual relations may be considered as ripe for critical analysis. Not only may organisational romance shape organisational artefacts, it also affect the identities of those who are situated within the field. However, freeing organisational phenomena from the oppression of rationalism, sex at work can not only be seen as disrupting the myth of objectivity, but perceived as something which is enjoyable and can serve to subvert the "seriousness" ascribed to organisational life (Hancock and Tyler, 2001). In entering into a relationship neither sanctioned nor formally recognised by the organisation, individuals may be viewed as creating an organisational identity which is not dictated to, or conferred by, larger bodies of power. Indeed, in entering into a relationship neither for organisational means or wider social pressures of reproduction, employees may be understood as engaging in what Giddens (1992, p. 147) calls "plastic sexuality... sex detached from its age-old subservience to differential power".

However, as yet, there is little evidence of how employees themselves construct workplace romance as an organisational phenomena or how it impinges on their own workplace identity. To further develop these ideas, the chapter now turns to the empirically driven analysis.

4. Introduction to Research Study and Methodology

To address the above research issues, the bar industry was chosen as a prospective research site. The UK pub industry employees over half a million people in over 60,000 public houses (Keynote, 2005). The research commenced after approaching and negotiating access with a large chain of pubs employing around 80,000 staff. The branding of the bar targeted the 18–35 youth market, and was mirrored in the demographics of their workforce, with around 65% of weekly salaried workers being under the age of 35. The chains shared a number of problems endemic to the industry, such as high turnover of staff, which had lead to a number of practices and incentives designed to create a strong cohesive culture within each house. For example, working evening or unsociable shifts meant that staff would socialise together after a late shift, drinking after work. Management would also organise inter-bar competitions or incentives to meet targets, which would be rewarded by money to spend on works nights out. All these incentives and aspects of working appeared conducive to fostering workplace romances.

Taped interviews were conducted with 48 employees and managers, following codes of confidentiality and ethical guidelines. Using a 5-point scale, participants were asked the extent to which they disagreed or agreed with a number of statements and why, their reasoning providing a basis for discussion. Participants were then asked a number of open-ended questions about whether they had experienced or witnessed organisational romance, their views on workplace relationships, and its role in organisational life. Rather than probing for a definitive answer, the interviews were understood as "guided conversations" (McNeill, 1990) where both the participants and the researcher had the opportunity to develop certain themes that did not explicitly come up in the questions. On transcribing the interviews, data were anonymised by assigning a number and the letters A–D to managers, and W to workers.

The interviews were subsequently analysed using a number of qualitative coding techniques, with particular interest in narrative analysis techniques in order to explore the personal stories and experiences of the participants. Due to the relative infancy of the research area, in the very early stages of analysis the authors favoured a grounded form of analysis where themes and codes were solely derived from the data, rather than preliminarily drawn up from other studies. Then the authors began to identify themes, which were further informed by both the research questions and our literature review. Transcripts were read several times by both authors independently, in order to allow themes to emerge, and were then compared against the other researcher's analysis and arranged into a number of larger conceptual categories. Once this stage was complete, we turned to techniques developed from narrative analysis, serving to explore the process of retelling an event as both a strategic and interpretative event in itself (Boje, 2001). This enabled us to move from the core beliefs being presented or upheld, to understanding the processes which were employed to support these ideals. Stories of organisational romance were thus seen in two ways. First, the experiences were understood as ways of supporting the legitimacy of beliefs espoused by participant throughout the interviews. Second, they were employed as a way of justifying conflicting or paradoxical opinions produced by the participant. As a means of achieving legitimacy, a number of techniques were also employed within the participants stories. These were identified as "effects of ideology" (Alvesson and Deetz, 2000, p. 84) which included: naturalisation of social order; universalisation of common interest and silencing of conflicting interest; domination of instrumental reasoning and; hegemonic processes. These stages of analysis allowed a set of key conceptual ideas to be developed relating to the constitution of organisational romance and its situated meaning in the workplace, and possible consequences. As a result of analysis, the findings are separated into three sections, subsequently dealing with the normalisation of organisational romance; the rules of engagement, and the gendered outcomes of organisational romance.

5. Normalising Organisational Romance

Whether participants agreed or disagreed with workplace romance, there was a consensus that it was a common occurrence. One of the key resources deployed by participants in justifying this was the specific work context. A young workforce, mostly single, were working together during evenings and weekends, and set aside times for socialising. Drawing on Gidden's (1992) notion of "plastic sexuality", the work environment was seen as creating playful landscapes. For example, one employee compared it to being at school: "Play-ground romances, oh, I'm going to kiss them, oh I'm going to take them home. No one takes it too seriously" (A4). Estimates of how often romance involvement varied from half the staff (C2, C4) to the majority or nearly all the staff (WB008, B3) and sought to emphasise the commonality of romance, serving to normalise the incidence of workplace romance.

Flirting was not confined to inter-staff relationships, but was strongly connected with the landscape of work: the pub. "People come to the pub to meet people or try and pull, so the bar staff are all included in that experience" (WC005). Rather than accentuate the divide between those working and not-working in the same space, participants concentrated on their role as creating an atmosphere or setting conducive to romance. Not only was this an enjoyable atmosphere to be in but was also "part of the sales technique at the end of the day" (WB009). This allusion to emotional labour (Hochschild, 1983, 1996), where work processes required individuals to express or provide an emotionally appealing appearance, was particularly common when justifying the occurrence of inter-staff romance. This requirement of the job not only created a space where flirting, humor, and sexual banter were acceptable features of the work landscape, but where emotional support between staff was needed in order to cope with the demands of dealing with drunkenness, fights, and unwanted sexual advances from customers.

Yet, workplace romance were also discussed as normal within any workplace environment, justified by participants drawing on a discourse upholding the social biologisation of human interaction. By forefronting attraction as an instinctual dynamic, interviewees were able to justify organisational romance as not simply common, but unavoidable. Due to "human instinct" (A2), "people are going to be attracted to each other no matter what" (WC004).

The effect this had on the participants' own work identity was noticeable through an absence of separation between their work and home personas. First, there was a "spatial overlapping" of work and social spheres, where the environment in which they were employed was also a space which they would occupy outside work. The labour processes also required emotions to be explicitly performed, or managed, and was not seen as incompatible with being professional or carrying out your work; indeed, it constituted part of being a good barperson. As well as drawing on these modes of justification, romance was also regarded as a "natural" aspect of any type of interaction, within the workplace or otherwise.

6. The "Rules of Engagement"

Unlike in other studies, the definition of organisational romance was by no means assumed or fixed, although was always seen as involving reciprocal relations, which distanced any "romantic" activities from harassment of unrequited advances. However, some participants, found the term "romance" misleading. Flirting, kissing, one-night stands, flings, and longer relationships were all seen under the rubric of "workplace" romance, although the participants were keen to emphasise that traditional conceptions of romance as associated with love or intimacy was not entirely suited to describe the one-off drunken encounters after a staff night out.

Despite this discrepancy, it appeared that there was a collective notion of what was acceptable and unacceptable in a nonplatonic workplace relationship. In this aspect, participants were more likely to recall stories of how *not* to conduct a romance. Again, this was based on the ideal of organisational romance as something which was light-hearted and enjoyable, providing entertainment for the whole team. While some stories recalled couples trying to keep their relationship a secret, this was seen as impossible, with many other employees guessing that the couples were involved long before it was revealed. In some sense, the relationship was often discussed as "belonging" to the whole team, and not simply involving the two people who were romantically attached. To legitimise this, participants discussed how the work group were all affected, whether through swapping shifts so the couple worked and had time off together, or allowing them to go on their breaks at the same time (WD002; WB004).

Staff leaving was a cause of concern for managers, either due to inter-hierarchical relationships: "She found it hard being ordered about by someone she was sleeping with and being treated the same as the rest of the bar staff" (D3), or dissolved relationships. What was interesting in the latter case was a lack of a "victim" figure: whether relationships had finished under acrimonious or amicable terms, both parties were expected to continue working productively. One employee (WB009) stated that they were caught between sympathising and having to "pretend you don't know anything and keep quiet", while others recall "morning-after awkwardness" (A4), and "tension and bitchiness" (B3). However, the negative effects from both good and bad relationships should be kept to a minimum and not affect the rest of the team. As such, sex was placed in contradictory positions as being both an integral and normal aspect of work, and yet not allowed to have a negative impact in any way.

Similarly, there appeared to be some shared consensus over management approaches to consensual romantic relationships at work. The company had no formal policy on how to deal with romance (as far as the manager and employees were aware of), and the possible introduction of such guidelines was met with cynicism, or claims that it was immoral to sanction such rules, stating it would just be "another of their rules we ignored" (A8). As a result, managers dealt with each instance on a case by case basis.

Of interest is the how participants discussed the line between when to intervene and when to sanction or ignore a relationship. The first-hand experiences of participants suggested that the majority of affairs were allowed to continue, with workers being allowed a degree of autonomy about how they chose to conduct work relations. However, this did not serve to counteract the importance of economic discourses and both managers and employees stated intervention should occur if the romance affected productivity in any way. Employing an economic marker contrasted strongly with the tone of previous discussions about romance, which were characterised by light-hearted, playful rhetoric. However, it remains unclear as to how any economic downturns of issue of productivity were attributed directly to a workplace romance, and managers avoided specific quantified examples.

Instead, managers discussed their own experiences of intervening as "sensing" or "feeling" that something was going wrong. As such, the decision to intervene remained a subjective judgment made by the managers.

Interestingly, this economic rationale was used to justify a number of practices that appeared on the surface as constituting unequal or discriminatory practice. One gay employee (WD003) found her girlfriend banned from coming into the put as she "looked like a lesbian... and that was the wrong kind of clientele". This action was justified as "bad for business" by drawing on the brand target, rather than homophobia. Similarly, negative tales of romance causing a detrimental affect were aligned with individuals who were lazy (WB006), not doing their work (WA005), or stole from the till (A3). Such cases of affected productivity were absent from stories emphasising the positive aspects of organisational romance, and appeared than the "bad effects" of workplace romance only arose from "bad employees".

7. Gendered Outcomes of Organisational Romance

As discussed above, of noted importance to the construction of organisational romance was the lack of a "victim" figure. No matter whether the dissolution of a relationship was mutual, or had involved a third party, those concerned were expected to not let it affect their workplace relations or efficiency. However, this did not mean that "everyone was a winner". Both the beliefs participants expressed about workplace romance, and through the assumptions and positioning of subject-actors within their stories, women were continually marginalised and presented as "losing" when it came to romantic relationships at work. While the pattern appeared that the more junior member of staff was most likely to leave if a relationship dissolved, one female manager (A7) stated it would always be the woman "as she is more likely to be criticised by the rest of the team". Similarly, the tales of managing the termination of a romance often focused on the women, or "girls", not being able to cope, and breaking down in the workplace. When discussing this moment of relationship breakdown, stories also relied heavily of gendered stereotypes of behaviours where the over-emotional party was invariably female, compared to the "coping" male: "They're (men are) not fussy, because they can get on with life without women anyway whereas women are called a slag (slang insult for women with loose morals) and are seen to not be able to separate their private life with anything else in their life" (WA006). From this it is clear that while emotions are normalised as workplace activity *being* emotional in itself was rejected as an acceptable working identity.

Women assumed a second position with narratives of organisational romance. The women were often presented as participating in the romance for pragmatic reasons. One manager (C4) discussed a "conniving" member of staff who received favourable shifts and treatment after an affair with one of the managers, while employees (such as WC002) discussed another employee "trying to get in or further up the company". Even though inter-hierarchical relationships where the male was the subordinate were also recalled by participants, these were not discussed regarding any degree of instrumentality.

The termination or commencement of a workplace relationship also appeared to have more immediate consequences on the women's working identity. One worker (WB004) stated that women were portrayed as "less fun once she is in a relationship" while others were well aware of the danger of being seen as a slag (WA006), slut (WA007), or tart (WD001) if they participated in two or more romances over a short period of time (WD001). On the other hand, such negative comments were absent when discussing the perceptions of men engaging in workplace relationships. Instead, they were the "lads", "studs", "heroes", or "the man". Although the double standard was well recognised by both the male and female participants, there was little evidence that they were actively challenged or refuted. While it was often conceded that the comments made were good-natured, attempts to answer back or challenge the remarks were not advisable: "people will think you can't take a joke" (WD001).

In this sense, women were bound to either comply with the double standards, as found in other discussions of romantic relationships (Giddens, 1994), or face accusations of threatening the "fun environment". With the norm of workplace romance defined and determined through a notion of "fun", anyone not complying with such rules will suffer the consequences. In doing so, the rules of organisational romance remained implicitly gendered where women are dichotomised through a Madonna–Whore complex. This means that women must either be classified as unable to control her emotions and manage "romantic love" and "working" as simultaneous activities, or defined through their perceived use of sexual manipulation and predatory behaviour to their own advantage. With both male and female participants relying on these norms to construct their views about workplace romance, it may be argued that the dominance of the "male in the head" (Holland *et al.*, 1994) acts as a regulating medium to assume a logic of patriarchy. In doing so, the rational emotional objective of the male is set as the norm, leaving feminised behaviour to be marginalised as "unsuitable".

8. Conclusion

In light of the lack of empirical-based evidence surrounding the real-life experiences of organisational romance by those who participate or witness them, this study set out to explore how inter-workplace relationship were defined, characterised, and understood by those who have to manage and encounter them in their daily working lives. While some discussion may be attributed to the particular context and labour processes within the public house industry, the rise in contingent workforces and the service-based job market suggests that the processes of justifying a "fun" working atmosphere may result in similar sentiments across a number of occupations.

Moreover, the processes of rationalisation and justification used by the participants draw on wider discourses about behavioural norms or treatment in relation to both the workplace, and social ideals. Romance is seen as an inevitable outcome of a close-knit workgroup, presented through the "voice of nature" (Barthes, 1977; Potter, 1996), where behaviour is viewed as beyond the individuals control; it is a "natural" part of human interactions. Yet, despite this, the rules of conduct are drawn up through the reliance on neo-economic measures, such as productivity, even through these are subjectively implemented in practice. Similarly, individuals are required to maintain their productivity and professionalism, both during and after the romance. Indeed, it appears that while romance is at first classified as a workplace phenomenon that should escape formal rules of regulations, participants constantly returned to the importance of conducting the relationship in ways that are typically associated with traditional bureaucratic modes of behaviour. In doing so, not only can the "façade of fun" be refuted, but this perspective served to shape the rules of organisational romance in distinctly gendered ways.

This research is by no means without its limitations. The research context may have created some bias in terms of the frequency or openness of employees in talking about romance, or the managers' apparent liberal attitudes to inter-staff relations. Similarly, the discussion of gay relationships suggests that there are distinct hetero-biases in what is deemed acceptable and unacceptable which need further study. However, it does raise a number of questions over how we discuss organisational romance, both as academic researchers, and as members of organisations. If, as this research suggests, romances are to occur whether sanctioned or not, it is clearly a workplace dimension that needs to be at least discussed as a management issue. Yet, by discussing an activity which sits outside hierarchy, job descriptions and workplace processes, it is difficult to see how a managerial rule could be applied without infringing on the civil liberties of their workforce. Nonetheless, as shown in this chapter, both employees and managers are well aware of the ability to create a consensus to prevent any disruption and maximise the positive outcomes of organisational romance, and are engaged in this negotiation at a local level, often without guidance from institutional or organisational bodies. Whether this can be achieved without the risk of reproducing inequalities is of course, another matter.

References

Alfred Marks Bureau (1991). *Meeting Your Partner at Work: A Quantitative Report on the Frequency and Effects of Relationships at Work*. Borehamwood: Alfred Marks Bureau.

Alvesson, M (2002). *Postmodernism and Social Research*. Buckingham: Open University Press.

Alvesson, M and S Deetz (2000). *Doing Critical Management Research*. London: Sage.

Anderson, CJ and PL Hunsaker (1985). Why there's romancing at the office and why it's every-one's problem. *Personnel*, 62(2), 57–63.

Barthes, R (1977). *Image, Music, Text*. London: Fontana.

Boje, DM (2001). *Narrative Methods for Organizational and Communication Research*. London: Sage.

Brewis, J and SA Linstead (2000). *Sex, Work and Sex Work*. London: Routledge.

Collins, E (1983). Managers and Lovers. *Harvard Business Review*, 61(5), 142–153.

Entwistle, J (2002). The aesthetic economy: The production of value in the field of fashion modeling. *Journal of Consumer Culture* 2(3), 317–340.

Fisher, AB (1994). Getting comfortable with couples in the workplace. *Fortune*, 130(7), 138–143.

Ford, RC and FS McLaughlin (1987). Should Cupid come to the workplace? An ASPA survey. *Personnel Administrator*, October, pp. 100–110.

Giddens, A (1992). *The Transformation of Intimacy: Sexuality, Love and Eroticism in Modern Societies*. Cambridge: Polity Press.

Giddens, A (1994). Men, women and romantic love. In *The Polity Reader in Gender Studies*, pp. 240–248 Oxford: Basil Blackwell.

Girvan, L (1995). A study of consensual sexual "misbehavior" in three distinctly work organizations. MBA dissertation, Edinburgh University Management School, Edinburgh.

Greenberg, JA (1987). A taxonomy of organizational justice theories. *Academy of Management Review*, 12, 9–22.

Gutek, BA (1989). Sexuality in the workplace key issues in social research and organisational practice. In *The Sexuality of Organisations*, J Hearn, D Sheppard, P Tancred-Sheriff and G Burrell (eds.), pp. 29–44, London: Sage.

Hancock, P and M Tyler (2001). *Work, Postmodernism and Organisation: A Critical Introduction*. London: Sage.

Harrison, R and R Lee (1986). Love at work. *Personnel Management*, January 20–24.

Hearn, J and W Parkin (1987). *"Sex" at "Work": The Power and Paradox of Organizational Sexuality*. Brighton: Wheatsheaf.

Hochschild, AR (1983). *The Managed Heart: The Commercialization of Human Feeling*. Berkeley, CA: University of California Press.

Hochschild, AR (1996). The emotional geography of work and family life. In *Gender Relations in Public and Private*, L Morris (ed.), pp. 13–32. New York: St Martin's Press.

Holland, J, C Ramazanoglu, S Sharpe and R Thomson (1994). Reputations: Journeying into gendered power relations. Paper presented at British Sociological Association Conference, Preston.

Karl, KA and CL Sutton (2000). An examination of the perceived fairness of workplace romance policies. *Journal of Business and Psychology*, 14(3), 429–442.

KeyNote Market Reports Plus (2005). Public Houses, KeyNote Ltd, Middlesex.

Lees, S (1993). *Sugar and Spice: Sexuality and Adolescent Girls*. Harmondsworth: Penguin.

Mainiero, LA (1986). A review and analysis of power dynamics in organizational romances. *Academy of Management Review*, 11, 750–762.

Mainiero, LA (1993). Dangerous Liaisons? A review of current issues concerning male and female romantic relationships in the workplace. In *Women in Management*, EA Fagenson (ed.), pp. 162–185. Newbury Park, CA, Sage.

McNeill, P (1990). *Research Methods*. London: Routledge.

Pierce, CA and H Aguinis (1997). Bridging the gap between romantic relationships and sexual harassment in organizations. *Journal of Organizational Behavior*, 18, 197–200.

Pierce, CA, D Byrne and H Aguinis (1996). Attraction in organizations: A model of workplace romance. *Journal of Organizational Behavior*, 17, 5–32.

Pierce, CA, H Aguinis and SK Adams (2000). Effects of a dissolved workplace romance and rater characteristics on responses to a sexual harassment accusation. *Academy of Management Journal*, 43, 869–880.

Potter, J (1996). *Representing Reality: Discourse, Rhetoric and Social Construction*. London: Sage.

Powell, GN (2000). Workplace romance in the public sector: Sex differences in reactions to the Clinton–Lewinsky affair. *Psychological Reports*, 87, 1043–1049.

Powell, GN and S Foley (1998). Something to talk about: Romantic relationships in organizational setting. *Journal of Management*, 24, 421–448.

Quinn, R (1977). Coping with Cupid: The formation, impact and management of romantic relationships in organizations. *Administrative Science Quarterly*, 22, 30–45.

Roy, D (1974). Sex in the factory: Informal heterosexual relations between supervisors and work groups. In *Deviant Behavior*, CD Bryant (ed.), pp. 44–66. Chicago: R and McNally.

Sanders, T (2005). Just acting: Sex workers' strategies for capitalising on sexuality. *Gender, Work and Organization*, 14(4), 319–342.

Society for Human Resource Management (1998). Workplace Romance Survey (item no. 62.17014). SHRM Public Affairs Department, Alexandria, VA.

Smith, ER, MA Becker, D Byrne and DP Przybyla (1993). Sexual attitudes of males and females as predators of interpersonal attraction and marital compatibility. *Journal of Applied Social Psychology*, 23(13), 1011–1034.

Training and Development Journal (1994). Are office romances OK (FaxForum results), 48(5), 38.

Trethaway, A (1999). Disciplined bodies, women's embodied identities at work. *Organisation Studies*, 20(3), 423–450

Tyler, M and P Abbott (1998). "Chocs away": Weight watching in the contemporary airline industry. *Sociology*, 32(3), 433–450.

Warfield, A (1987). Co-worker romances: Impact on the work group and on career oriented women. *Personnel*, 64(5), 22–35.

Weber, M. (1948). *From Max Weber: Essays in Sociology*, HH Gerth and CW Mills, (eds.). London: Routledge.

Wilson, RJ, C Filosa and A Fennel (2003). Romantic relationships at work: Does privacy trump the dating police? *Defense Counsel Journal*, 70(1), 78–89.

2

AN APPLICATION OF EXTREME VALUE THEORY IN MODELLING EXTREME SHARE RETURNS

Konstantinos Tolikas

Cardiff University, UK

Extreme value theory (EVT) methods are used to investigate the asymptotic distribution/s of the extreme minima and maxima of the Athens Stock Exchange daily returns over the period 1976–2001. Innovative aspects of this study include: (1) the generalised extreme value and generalised logistic distributions are considered, (2) L-moments ratio diagrams are used to identify the distribution/s most likely to fit the extreme daily returns adequately, (3) the probability weighted moments method is used to estimate the parameters of the distribution/s, and (4) the Anderson–Darling goodness of fit test is employed to test the adequacy of fit. The generalised logistic distribution is found to provide adequate descriptions of the behaviour of both the extreme minima and maxima over the period studied; however, the asymptotic distributions of extremes appear to become less fat-tailed over time, implying that the probability of a large daily return occurring is decreasing.

Keywords: Extreme value theory; L-moments; Anderson–Darling goodness of fit test; Generalised extreme value distribution; generalised logistic distribution.

1. Introduction

Longin (1996) defined the extreme return of an index to be the maximum or minimum return over a pre-specified time period; for example, the minimum daily return over a period of one week. These extremes can be the result of market corrections that can be characterised as usual market conditions or the results of political, economic, social, speculative or other unknown causes that can be characterised as market crises. Such large stock price movements can lead to enormous losses and consequently financial managers and regulators are increasingly interested in their associated probabilities. For example, the Bank for International Settlements (BIS, 1996) stipulated the use of value-at-risk (VaR)[1] as a market risk measurement tool for financial institutions to calculate minimum capital requirements (MCR). This MCR aims to cover the potential losses that might accrue from a financial institution's market positions due to adverse market movements and should, therefore, help to avoid financial disasters. A usual assumption made in estimating VaR is that financial returns follow a normal distribution. Empirical evidence, however, suggests that most of the times, financial return distributions, especially those of high frequency (i.e., intraday or daily returns), deviate from normality (see, for example, Aparicio and Estrada (2001) for an assessment of the normality assumption of European stock returns). In this case the probabilities of extreme returns occurring will be underestimated and that can have a severe impact on investment strategies and on the stability of the financial system.

On the other hand, extreme value theory (EVT) is a special branch of statistics that focuses exclusively on these extremes and is increasingly used to model financial returns that exhibit non-normal behaviour. The aim of this chapter is to examine the usefulness of innovative EVT methods by analysing the asymptotic distribution of the extreme minima and maxima daily returns of a developing stock market; the Athens Stock Exchange (ASE). For that reason, daily prices of the ASE general index for the period 1976–1988 have been manually collected from the ASE Records Department and combined with daily prices for the period 1988–2001 collected from Datastream. This is a period of sufficient length to include major changes in the ASE as it has developed over the last decades. In addition, the EVT methods used in this chapter are quite innovative in financial analysis and their usefulness has not yet fully explored. Therefore, it also aims to introduce a new toolkit for those interested in the analysis of the extremal behaviour of financial returns.

This chapter introduces a number of innovative points with respect to current applications of EVT in finance. First, in addition to the generalised

---

[1]VaR can be defined as the maximum loss of a portfolio over a particular time horizon and at a pre-specified confidence level (Jorion, 2000). Statistically, it can be defined as one of the lowest quantiles of the distribution of returns.

extreme value (GEV) distribution, the generalised logistic (GL) is also considered as a model for the extremes of the ASE daily returns. Second, the distribution/s that are likely to best fit the empirical data are identified by using L-moments ratio diagrams and the parameters of these distributions are estimated by using the probability weighted moments (PWM) method. Finally, the Anderson–Darling (AD) test statistic is then used to test the goodness of fit of the chosen distribution/s to the empirical data.

This chapter is divided by the following sections. Section 2 provides a brief review of the literature regarding the EVT. The methodological steps are described in Section 3, while Section 4 describes the ASE general index daily returns. In Section 5, empirical results are obtained and the most likely distributions to fit adequately the extreme returns are identified. Finally, Section 6 concludes and summarises the chapter.

2. Extreme Value Theory

Longin (1996) was one of the first to apply EVT in finance. In his seminal work he identified the distribution for the extreme daily returns of the S&P500 over the period 1885–1990 to be the GEV. He also argued that EVT could be useful in VaR estimation, margin setting in future markets, and in regulating capital requirements for financial institutions. The GEV distribution was also found by McNeil (1999) to model adequately the S&P500 annual minima during the period 1960–1987 who also illustrated that the drop of the S&P500 index in the October 1987 crash could have been predicted. Cotter (2001) applied EVT in estimating margin requirements in future markets and argued that EVT can lead to more realistic estimates. More recently Gettinby *et al.* (2004) investigated the distribution of the daily extreme returns in the UK stock market and found that the GL distribution provides accurate descriptions of both the minima and maxima extremes. Tolikas *et al.* (2007) also found that the GL distribution describes well the extremal behaviour of daily returns in the German stock market and they also provided evidence that EVT can be useful in risk management since it can lead to more accurate VaR estimates. Important papers wherein the role of EVT in financial management is emphasised both theoretically and empirically, include Longin (2000), McNeil and Frey (2000) and Embrechts *et al.* (1998). A detailed description of the theory of extremes and its applications can be found in the books by Embrechts *et al.* (1997).

3. Methodology

The EVT methods proposed in this study involve a number of steps. First, the frequency of financial returns should be chosen. This is influenced by the liquidity of the financial assets and since a general stock market index is used, daily logarithmic returns are employed. Second, the length of the selection interval over which the extremes are collected has to be specified. This choice directly affects the number of minima and maxima that are available for the analysis and should be sufficiently large to allow for the efficient estimation of the parameters of the extremes distribution. This is an arbitrary choice and in order to investigate both the behaviour of parameters and the goodness of fit over successively increasing selection intervals; weekly, monthly, and quarterly extremes are considered. Without lost of generality, these extremes are collected over non-overlapping periods 5, 20, and 60 trading days, respectively. The behaviour of the extremes distribution over time aggregation is also examined by dividing the series of weekly and monthly extremes into 2, 4, and 10 sub-periods and the quarterly extremes into 2 and 4 sub-periods.

The third step is to identify the distributions that are likely to model the empirical data adequately. The choice of an appropriate distribution may be affected by criteria such as its ability to reproduce the variability of the empirical data, sensitivity to data outliers, computational complexity, and the number of parameters to be estimated (Cunnane, 1985). Inspired by the work in the flood frequency analysis area, it was decided to focus on the GEV and GL distributions. Details of these distributions can be found in Appendix A. There are three parameter distributions that have been proved particularly effective in describing stochastic processes of extreme observations in environmental and engineering studies (see, for example, Peel *et al.*, 2001). The parameters of these distributions are commonly referred as the location (β), scale (α), and shape (κ). The location and scale parameters are analogous to the mean and standard deviation, while the shape parameter is directly linked to the fatness of tails of the empirical distribution. Higher, in absolute terms, shape parameter values correspond to fatter tailed distributions and vice versa. Although the GEV has already been used to analyse financial extreme returns, the GL has only been used in a limited number of studies (Gettinby *et al.*, 2004; Tolikas *et al.*, 2007). This set of distributions includes as special cases stochastic processes such as, the normal, student-t, log-logistic and log-normal distributions, mixture of normal distributions or even ARCH processes (de Haan *et al.*, 1989).

The most likely distributions to fit the extremes are identified by using L-moment ratio diagrams. L-moments are linear combinations of ordered data and analogously to conventional moments they provide a summary statistic for probability distributions.[2] The main advantage of the L-moments is that being linear combinations of the ordered data they are more robust than the conventional moments in the presence of outliers[3] (Hosking, 1990; Royston, 1992; Sankarasubramanian and Srinivasan, 1999). They defined for any random variable X which mean exists as follows (Hosking, 1990):

$$\lambda_r \equiv r^{-1} \sum_{k=0}^{r-1} (-1)^k \binom{r-1}{k} EX_{r-k:r}, \quad r = 1, 2, \ldots . \tag{1}$$

The first two L-moments, λ_1 and λ_2, can be regarded as measures of location and scale of a distribution. Additionally, the quantities $\tau_r = \lambda_r/\lambda_2$, where $r = 3, 4, \ldots$ are called the L-moment ratios of the random variable X and the first two, τ_3 and τ_4, can be regarded as measures of skewness and kurtosis, respectively. The identification of the distributions that best fit the empirical data is implemented graphically by using a statistical distribution map, wherein the L-moment ratios equivalent to skewness and kurtosis are estimated from the data and plotted.[4] The same diagram contains the plots of the skewness and kurtosis of the theoretical distributions which are considered. The identification of the appropriate distribution for a particular data set is made, by choosing the distribution whose L-skewness and L-kurtosis curve passes closest to it. This allows the examination of the suitability of many distributions in just one diagram. For the purpose of distributions identification, the utility and the superiority of L-moment ratio diagrams against conventional moments diagrams is well illustrated in Peel *et al.* (2001) and Pandey *et al.* (2001).

The next step is to estimate the parameters of these most appropriate distributions. For that purpose the method of PWM is used. PWM are expectations of certain functions of a random variable X with distribution function F, whose mean exists, and they were first defined by Greenwood *et al.*

---

[2]The book by Hosking and Wallis (1997) provides a detailed presentation of the L-moments theory.

[3]This is because the calculation of conventional moments, like skewness and kurtosis, involve third and fourth powers; thus, greater weight is given to outliers.

[4]Graphical methods have been used for a long time in social sciences to examine the goodness of fit of a theoretical distribution to the empirical data and have found to be particularly useful.

(1979). A tractable definition is given by Hosking (1986):

$$\alpha_r = E[X\{1 - F(X)\}^r], \quad r = 0, 1, \ldots, \tag{2}$$

where $E[X(\cdot)]$ is the expectation of the quantile function of a random variable X. The PWM method estimates a distribution's parameters by equating the sample moments to those of the fitted distribution. In the case of small samples this method is considered to be more efficient compared to the maximum likelihood (ML) method (Coles and Dixon, 1999). This is particularly important since, by definition, extremes are rare; even long observational periods can provide very few data points if, for example, annual minima are used. PWM are linearly related to L-moments by the following relationships (Hosking, 1986):

$$\lambda_1 = \alpha_0, \tag{3}$$

$$\lambda_2 = \alpha_0 - 2\alpha_1, \tag{4}$$

$$\lambda_3 = \alpha_0 - 6\alpha_1 + 6\alpha_2, \tag{5}$$

$$\lambda_4 = \alpha_0 - 12\alpha_1 + 30\alpha_2 - 20\alpha_3, \tag{6}$$

Hosking *et al.* (1985) showed that for the GEV distribution, estimates of parameters and quantiles made using the PWM method are estimated with at least 70% efficiency. They also showed that for shape parameter values in the range -0.5 to 0.5 and for samples of up to 100 observations, estimates generated by the PWM method have lower root-mean square error than estimates generated by the ML method. Additionally, Landwehr *et al.* (1979) found that for a special case of the GEV distribution, the Gumbel, the PWM method results in more efficient parameter estimates compared to the ML and conventional moments method.

Once the appropriate distribution/s have been identified and the parameters have been estimated it is essential to test the goodness of fit of the chosen distribution/s to the empirical data. Anderson and Darling (1954) defined a class of test statistics by:

$$\int_{-\infty}^{\infty} [F_n(x) - F(x)]^2 \phi(x) dF(x), \tag{7}$$

where $F_n(x)$ is the empirical distribution function (EDF) of a random variable X, $F(x)$ is the cumulative distribution function (CDF) of X, n is the number of observations, and $\phi(x)$ is a function that assigns weight to the squared differences $[F_n(x) - F(x)]^2$. When, $\phi(x) = [F(x)(1 - F(x))]^{-1}$ the test statistic focuses on measuring discrepancies in both tails.[5] Stephens (1976) and d'Agostino and Stephens (1986) have reported that the AD goodness of fit test to be more powerful than the Pearson chi-squared test for small sample sizes.

4. Data Description

The dataset used to illustrate the usefulness of EVT consists of 6466 daily logarithmic returns[6] of the ASE general index that cover the 26-year period of 2 January 1976 to 28 December 2001. The data for the period 1976–1988 have been manually collected from the ASE Records Department while the data for the period 1988–2001 has been obtained from Datastream.[7] Prices for the second period take the account of any capital changes (e.g., dividend distributions, stock splits) but this is not the case for the prices of the first period. However, the focus is on the extreme returns which are collected over selection intervals and therefore, it can be reasonably assumed that any effect of capital changes is well diversified and no significant bias is present in the results.

Table 1 contains descriptive statistics of the dataset employed in the analysis. The ASE index has a daily mean return of 0.06% and a daily standard deviation of 1.64%. The minimum daily return[8] is −16.29% and occurred on 7/12/87 while the maximum, 24.23%, occurred two days after on 11/12/87. Furthermore, the daily returns distribution has a low value of skewness, 0.329, but a rather high value of kurtosis, 19.045. The kurtosis

---

[5]The AD test is a modification of the kolmogorov–Smirnoff goodness of fit test. However, the AD test depends on the particular distribution that is examined. This makes the AD a more effective test but it has the drawback that critical values must be produced by simulation.

[6]Daily logarithmic returns are calculated according to the formula, $X_t = 100 \ln(P_t/P_{t-1})$, where P_t is the index closing price at day t.

[7]Therefore, the dataset covers a period that computers were not used to record stock prices during which ASE prompted by EU directives as well as technological advances went considerable transformation. The Datastream code is TOTMKGR and the index is composed of the most heavily traded shares that aim to cover the 70–80% of the total market capitalisation.

[8]Although the ASE was closed around the period of the stock markets crash on 19/10/87, the negative sentiment of investors affected the Greek stock market which lost 13.51% on 26/10/87, 10.24% on 4/11/87, 12.77% on 26/11/87, and eventually 16.29% on 7/12/87.

Table 1. Descriptive statistics for ASE index daily returns and for the weekly, monthly, and quarterly minima over the period 1976–2001 and over the sub-periods 1976–1988 and 1989–2001.

	N	Return (%)	St. Dev (%)	Min (%)	Max (%)	Skewness	Kurtosis	Shapiro–Wilk	p-value
Period 1976–2001									
Daily	6466	0.063	1.644	−16.291	24.227	−0.329*	19.045*	0.906	<0.01
Minima									
Weekly	1293	−1.247	1.709	−16.291	3.114	−3.292*	16.438j	0.836	<0.01
Monthly	323	−2.461	2.471	−16.291	−0.089	−2.395*	7.185*	0.856	<0.01
Quarterly	107	−3.773	3.174	−16.291	−0.621	−1.638*	2.904*	0.905	<0.01
Maxima									
Weekly	1293	1.426	1.828	−2.277	24.227	3.465*	25.086*	0.853	<0.01
Monthly	323	2.716	2.593	0.103	24.227	2.922*	16.338*	0.873	<0.01
Quarterly	107	4.083	3.416	0.351	24.227	2.578*	11.271*	0.885	<0.01
Period 1976–1988									
Daily	3230	0.041	1.302	−16.291	24.227	0.786*	68.411*	0.781	<0.01
Minima									
Weekly	646	−0.783	1.559	−16.291	1.589	−5.704*	41.821*	0.690	<0.01
Monthly	161	−1.685	2.411	−16.291	−0.089	−4.103*	18.710*	0.702	<0.01
Quarterly	53	−2.816	3.398	−16.291	−0.621	−2.820*	7.767*	0.761	<0.01
Maxima									
Weekly	646	0.874	1.616	−2.258	24.227	6.789*	75.810*	0.706	<0.01
Monthly	161	1.821	2.570	0.103	24.227	5.117*	37.382*	0.723	<0.01
Quarterly	53	3.038	3.717	0.351	24.227	3.986*	20.372*	0.756	<0.01

(*Continued*)

Table 1. *(Continued)*

	N	Return (%)	St. Dev (%)	Min (%)	Max (%)	Skewness	Kurtosis	Shapiro–Wilk	p-value
Period 1989–2001									
Daily	3236	0.084	1.926	−12.426	15.311	0.149*	5.535*	0.964	<0.01
Minima									
Weekly	647	−1.710	1.728	−12.426	3.114	−2.049*	6.242*	0.907	<0.01
Monthly	162	−3.232	2.288	−12.426	−0.734	−1.415*	1.748*	0.922	<0.01
Quarterly	54	−4.711	2.646	−12.426	−1.101	−0.622	−0.223*	0.969	0.02
Maxima									
Weekly	647	1.976	1.863	−2.277	15.311	1.915*	6.811*	0.927	<0.01
Monthly	162	3.604	2.299	0.630	15.311	1.624*	4.636*	0.936	<0.01
Quarterly	54	5.109	2.761	1.387	15.311	1.360*	3.004*	0.949	<0.01

Note: N denotes the number of observations; St. Dev denotes the standard deviation of returns and the minimum and maximum returns are indicated as Min and Max. *Indicates statistical significance. The Shapiro–Wilk test examines the hypothesis that the daily and the extreme minima and maxima returns are normally distributed.

value indicate that the distribution of daily returns is fat-tailed and therefore, it deviates from normality.[9] This is also confirmed by the Shapiro–Wilk test statistic which rejects the normality assumption at the 99% confidence level.[10]

In addition to the whole time period, descriptive statistics of the ASE daily returns for the sub-periods, 1976–1988 and 1989–2001 are also reported in Table 1. The mean daily return for the period 1976–1988 was 0.04% while that for the period 1989–2001 was double that figure, 0.08%; however, standard deviation was also higher in the second period. Although skewness was low for both sub-periods, daily returns exhibited a large kurtosis of 68.41 in the first sub-period while in the second sub-period it was remarkably lower, 5.53. The normality hypothesis was also rejected for both sub-periods. A Q–Q plot where quantiles of the daily returns empirical distributions for the two sub-periods are plotted against those of a normal distribution highlights the differences between the empirical distributions of the daily returns in the two sub-periods[11] (Figure 1).

---

[9]The values of skewness and kurtosis for the normal distribution are 0 and 3, respectively.

[10]To examine further the distribution of the daily returns, returns are standardised and the pairs of empirical percentiles (1%, 99%), (5%, 95%), and (10%, 90%) are compared with those of the standard normal distribution; $(-2.326, 2.326)$, $(-1.645, 1.645)$, and $(-1.281, 1.281)$, respectively. The comparison reveals that the pair of (1%, 99%) empirical percentiles are too large, $(-3.102, 3.096)$, while the pairs of (5%, 95%), and (10%, 90%) are too small, $(-1.315, 1.490)$ and $(-0.842, 0.933)$, respectively. Additionally, if the ASE daily returns were normally distributed then only 18 of the 6466 observations would lie outside plus or minus three standard deviations from the mean. This is because a well-known property of the normal distribution is that the 99.73% of the observations lie within plus or minus 3 standard deviations away from the mean. Therefore, only the 0.27% of total observations lies outside that range and since the normal distribution is symmetric, there should be a proportion of 0.135% in each tail. However, there are 144 observations that lie outside this range; 67 observations in the left tail and 77 observations in the right tail. Clearly, the empirical distribution of ASE daily returns exhibits more extreme observations than those implied by the normal distribution.

[11]Furthermore, when the pairs of (1%, 99%), (5%, 95%), and (10%, 90%) empirical standardized percentiles are examined, it is revealed that for the period 1976–1988 all pairs are too small, $(-2.066, 2.278)$, $(-0.733, 0.880)$, and $(-0.468, 0.505)$, in comparison to those of the normal distribution; $(-2.326, 2.326)$, $(-1.645, 1.645)$, and $(-1.281, 1.281)$, respectively, while for the period 1989–2001 the pairs of (1%, 99%), (5%, 95%) are too large, $(-3.323, 3.325)$ and $(-1.707, 1.929)$ and the pair of (10%, 90%) is too small, $(-1.167, 1.280)$. Additionally, for the period 1976–1988, 59 observations lie outside the range of plus or minus 3 standard deviations, while only 9 are expected, with 27 in the left and 32 in the right tail of the empirical distribution. For the period 1989–2001 there are 54 observations outside that range, while only 9 are expected, with 25 in the left and 29 in the right tail of the empirical distribution.

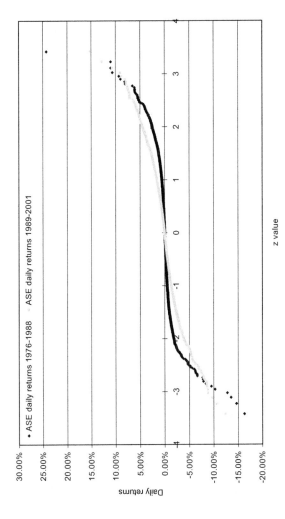

Figure 1.   ASE index daily returns Q–Q *plot* for the periods 1976–1988 and 1989–2001. In this figure quantiles of the empirical distributions are plotted against quantiles of the normal distribution. In case of normality a straight line is anticipated. It is clear that not only did the two distributions deviate from normality, they also differ considerably.

5.   Analysis of the Extreme Daily Returns

5.1.   *Identification of the appropriate distribution for the extreme daily returns*

Table 1 contains descriptive statistics for the weekly, monthly, and quarterly minima and maxima extreme daily returns which were collected over the 26-year period. The series of weekly and monthly extremes were also divided into 2, 4, and 10 sub-periods and the series of quarterly extremes into 2 and 4 sub-periods. The L-skewness (τ_3) and L-kurtosis (τ_4) were calculated and plotted for each of the sub-periods of the series of weekly, monthly, and quarterly extremes. The same diagram also contain the theoretical relationship between the L-skewness and L-kurtosis of different distributions.[12]

Figure 2 contains the plots of τ_3 and τ_4 for the 10 sub-periods of the weekly minima over the period 1976–2001. It can be noticed that the L-moment ratio points are mainly dispersed around the theoretical curves of the GL and the GEV distributions with most points lying above the GL curve. This is an interesting observation since higher L-kurtosis values correspond to fatter tailed distributions. Similar patterns appeared in the L-moment ratio diagrams for different sub-periods of the weekly, monthly, and quarterly minima.[13] The same graphical analysis was implemented for the extreme weekly, monthly, and quarterly maxima. Again, the L-moment ratio points are mainly dispersed around the theoretical curves of the GL and GEV distributions. Overall, although the L-moment ratio diagrams do not provide additional support in favour of either the GL or the GEV distribution the visual evidence suggests that the analysis should focus only on these two distributions.

5.2.   *Parameter estimation and goodness of fit test*

The whole series of the weekly minima as well as different sub-periods of the weekly minima were fitted by the GL and GEV distributions using the PWM method. Table 2 contains the parameter estimates and the AD goodness of fit test for the 10 sub-periods. It is noticeable that both the GEV

---

[12]A single point represents two parameter distributions (e.g., the normal), whereas a three parameter distribution is represented by a curve (e.g., the GEV). The lower bound of all the distributions is also plotted.

[13]These diagrams are not included in this chapter but they are available from the author upon request.

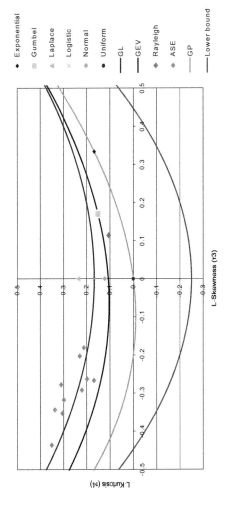

Figure 2. L-moment ratios diagram for the ASE index daily returns weekly minima for 10 sub-periods from 1976–2001. This figure illustrates the L-moment ratio points for the ASE index daily returns weekly minima divided into 10 sub-periods, over the period 1976–2001. The plots of L-skewness and L-kurtosis are mainly concentrated around the theoretical curves of the GL and the GEV distributions indicating that these two distributions are likely to fit adequately the empirical data.

Table 2. PWM parameter estimates and goodness of fit test for the fitted GEV and GL to the weekly minima of the ASE index for 1, 2, 4, and 10 sub-periods of the period 1976–2001.

Periods (n)	N	GEV estimates				GL estimates				Better fit
		β	α	κ	p-value	β	α	κ	p-value	
$n = 1$										
1	1293	0.005	0.007	−0.322	0.000	−0.008	0.006	0.394	0.000	None
$n = 2$										
1	647	0.002	0.004	−0.419	0.000	−0.004	0.004	0.470	0.000	None
2	646	0.009	0.010	−0.198	0.000	−0.013	0.007	0.304	0.005	GL
$n = 4$										
1	323	0.003	0.003	−0.273	0.000	−0.004	0.002	0.358	0.002	GL
2	323	0.003	0.006	−0.423	0.000	−0.005	0.005	0.473	0.000	None
3	323	0.009	0.009	−0.232	0.001	−0.013	0.007	0.328	0.030	GL
4	324	−0.018	0.017	0.866	0.000	−0.014	0.008	0.280	0.019	GL
$n = 10$										
1	129	0.003	0.003	−0.217	0.002	−0.004	0.002	0.317	0.083	GL
2	129	0.002	0.003	−0.253	0.000	−0.003	0.002	0.344	0.033	GL
3	129	0.003	0.004	−0.161	0.000	−0.005	0.003	0.278	0.001	GL
4	129	0.002	0.004	−0.266	0.004	−0.003	0.003	0.352	0.048	GL
5	129	0.005	0.011	−0.377	0.001	−0.010	0.009	0.436	0.003	GL
6	129	0.010	0.014	−0.182	0.311	−0.016	0.010	0.292	0.531	GL
7	129	0.010	0.008	−0.140	0.638	−0.013	0.006	0.263	0.722	GL
8	129	0.006	0.004	−0.017	0.069	−0.008	0.003	0.181	0.570	GL
9	129	0.010	0.013	−0.146	0.281	−0.015	0.009	0.267	0.158	GEV
10	132	0.013	0.011	−0.051	0.003	−0.017	0.008	0.203	0.060	GL

Note: This table includes the PWM parameter estimates and the Anderson–Darling goodness of fit test p-values for the GEV and GL distributions fitted to the weekly minima divided into 2, 4, and 10 sub-periods over the period 1976–2001. N denotes the number of observations, κ, α, β denote the shape, scale, and location parameters, respectively and p-value is the p-value of the Anderson–Darling test statistic.

and GL did not provide an adequate fit to the whole data series as well as when 2 and 4 sub-periods were used. This is probably because the nature of extremes distribution is changing over time and therefore, when large time-periods are used that encompass most of these changes the fitting becomes difficult. However, when 10 sub-periods were used the GL distribution fitted the empirical data adequately in six of the 10 sub-periods while the GEV in four of them. In comparison to the GEV, the GL fitted better the data in 9 of the 10 sub-periods. However, a point that should be added in favour of the GEV distribution is that it performed significantly better in the last sub-periods. This is probably because the distribution of extremes in the second half of the whole period is less fat-tailed than it is in the first half. Therefore, the GEV, which is less fat-tailed than the GL, improves its ability to fit the empirical data.

In Figure 3 one could notice that the estimated scale and location parameters of the GL distribution over time behave in a stable fashion for the first periods but become volatile for the next sub-periods. This is because the second half of the total period contains larger negative daily returns than the first half.[14] These large negative values probably reflect the effects of political uncertainty on the ASE during that period as well as the global volatile environment. In contrast, the shape parameter is more volatile in the first half than it is in the second half of the total period.

For the GEV distribution the parameters, in general, follow similar patterns (Figure 4). The scale and location parameters appear to be stable for almost all periods that represent the first half of the 26-year period. In addition, the shape parameter estimates for the GEV vary more than the estimates for the GL and this is especially the case for the first half of the total period. Overall, even though both the GL and the GEV distributions fail to fit the whole sample of weekly minima, the GL performed better than the GEV when sub-periods were used. Additionally, the parameter behaviour over time appeared to be more stable for the GL than the GEV distribution.

The weekly maxima of the whole interval as well as of 2, 4, and 10 sub-periods were also fitted by the GL and GEV distributions (Table 3).[15] Similarly, in the case of weekly minima both distributions failed to fit adequately the empirical data in the case of 1, 2, and 4 sub-periods. However, when the data was divided into 10 sub-periods both distributions improved

---

[14]For example, the second half of the whole period contains the large drops of the ASE index with values of −14.63% (3/10/88), −12.42% (16/10/89), and −10.59% (6/11/89), respectively.
[15]In the interest of brevity, these results are not included in the chapter.

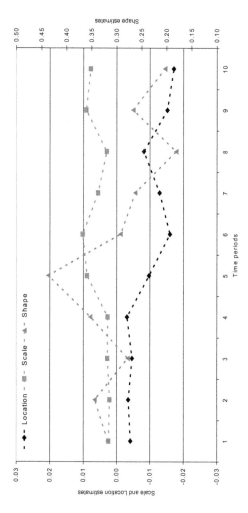

Figure 3. PWM parameter estimates for the GL for the case of weekly minima divided into 10 sub-periods. This figure illustrates the behaviour of the scale, location, and shape parameters over time for the GL distribution fitted to the series of weekly minima divided into 10 sub-periods.

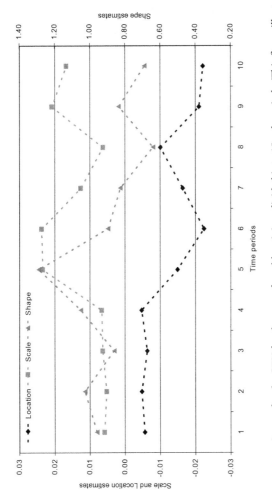

Figure 4. PWM parameter estimates for the GEV for the case of weekly minima divided into 10 sub-periods. This figure illustrates the behaviour of the scale, location, and shape parameters over time for the GEV distribution fitted to the series of weekly minima divided into 10 sub-periods.

their performance. In particular, the GL fitted adequately in 7 of the sub-periods while the GEV in the last 5. It is noticeable that these 5 sub-periods refer to the period after 1988. An explanation is that the distribution of the ASE daily returns became less fat-tailed in the second half of the period examined, thus the GEV improved its ability to fit adequately extreme daily returns. In terms of parameters' behaviour over time, the patterns seem to be similar to those found in the case of weekly minima. For both the GL and GEV distributions, the location and scale parameters behave stable in the first half of the whole interval and they become volatile in the second half. Additionally, the shape parameter tends to take larger values, in absolute terms, in the first half rather than the second. Since larger shape parameter values in absolute terms indicate fatter tails it could be argued that the empirical distribution of the ASE index weekly maxima becomes less fat-tailed over time. This finding can be interpreted as implying that the probability of a large extreme maxima occurring has decreased after 1988.

Overall both the GL and the GEV distributions appear to be able to provide an adequate fit to the empirical data. However, the GL seems to be the most appropriate distribution for the ASE extreme daily returns since its ability to fit the empirical data adequately is more consistent over time.

5.3.   *GL and GEV parameter estimates behaviour over time aggregation*

The monthly and quarterly minima and maxima of the ASE index were also fitted by the GL and GEV distributions. The reason for doing that is if a distribution fits adequately the extremes then its behaviour should be consistent over different selection intervals of extremes. Results for the case of the monthly minima are presented in Table 4 and for the case of quarterly minima in Table 5. One could notice that none of the distributions fitted adequately the monthly minima for the whole period. In the case of 2 sub-periods the GEV fitted adequately in the first sub-period and the GL in none, while in the case of 4 sub-periods the GL fitted the data adequately in two while the GEV only in one sub-period. However, when the data was divided into 10 sub-periods both distributions performed better. The GEV fitted adequately in 6 and the GL in 7 sub-periods. In comparison, the GL fitted the data better than the GEV in 8 of the sub-periods. When quarterly minima were fitted by the GL and GEV both distributions failed to fit adequately the whole dataset while in the case of two sub-periods both the GEV and GL fitted adequately the data in the first sub-period with the GL giving a higher AD goodness of fit

Table 3. PWM parameters estimates and goodness of fit test for the fitted GEV and GL to the weekly maxima of the ASE index for 1, 2, 4 and 10 sub-periods of the period 1976–2001.

Periods (n)	N	GEV estimates				GL estimates				Better fit
		β	α	κ	p-value	β	α	κ	p-value	
n = 1										
1	1293	0.006	0.008	−0.301	0.000	0.009	0.007	−0.378	0.000	None
n = 2										
1	647	0.003	0.004	−0.438	0.000	0.005	0.004	−0.484	0.001	GL
2	646	0.011	0.012	−0.144	0.019	0.016	0.008	−0.266	0.009	GEV
n = 4										
1	323	0.002	0.003	−0.379	0.000	0.003	0.002	−0.438	0.001	GL
2	323	0.004	0.006	−0.402	0.000	0.007	0.005	−0.456	0.009	GL
3	323	0.010	0.011	−0.203	0.027	0.015	0.008	−0.307	0.063	GL
4	324	0.012	0.012	−0.075	0.045	0.017	0.008	−0.219	0.014	GEV
n = 10										
1	129	0.003	0.003	−0.378	0.000	0.004	0.003	−0.437	0.024	GL
2	129	0.001	0.003	−0.349	0.001	0.002	0.002	−0.415	0.008	GL
3	129	0.002	0.003	−0.350	0.000	0.003	0.003	−0.416	0.017	GL
4	129	0.003	0.004	−0.175	0.018	0.005	0.003	−0.287	0.470	GL
5	129	0.010	0.011	−0.325	0.000	0.015	0.009	−0.397	0.084	GL
6	129	0.015	0.017	−0.126	0.507	0.022	0.012	−0.254	0.581	GL
7	129	0.010	0.010	−0.093	0.265	0.014	0.007	−0.231	0.099	GEV
8	129	0.006	0.005	−0.104	0.730	0.009	0.004	−0.238	0.839	GL
9	129	0.016	0.015	0.023	0.764	0.022	0.009	−0.155	0.321	GEV
10	132	0.013	0.013	−0.014	0.523	0.018	0.009	−0.179	0.210	GEV

Note: This table includes the PWM parameter estimates and the Anderson–Darling goodness of fit test p-values for the GEV and GL distributions fitted to the weekly maxima divided into 2, 4, and 10 sub-periods over the period 1976–2001. N denotes the number of observations, κ, α, β denote the shape, scale, and location parameters, respectively and p-value is the p-value of the Anderson–Darling test statistic.

Table 4. PWM parameter estimates and goodness of fit test for the fitted GEV and GL to the monthly minima of the ASE index for 10 sub-periods for the period 1976–2001.

Periods (n)	N	GEV estimates				GL estimates				Better fit
		β	α	κ	p-value	β	α	κ	p-value	
$n = 1$										
1	323	0.013	0.010	−0.356	0.000	−0.017	0.008	0.420	0.003	GL
$n = 2$										
1	162	0.008	0.005	−0.552	0.097	−0.010	0.005	0.578	0.039	GEV
2	161	0.021	0.013	−0.219	0.001	−0.027	0.010	0.318	0.003	GL
$n = 4$										
1	80	0.007	0.003	−0.476	0.007	−0.008	0.003	0.515	0.103	GL
2	80	0.009	0.007	−0.524	0.275	−0.013	0.007	0.555	0.319	GL
3	80	0.020	0.012	−0.290	0.018	−0.025	0.010	0.370	0.028	GL
4	83	0.022	0.014	−0.133	0.002	−0.028	0.010	0.258	0.007	GL
$n = 10$										
1	32	0.007	0.003	−0.429	0.740	−0.009	0.003	0.477	0.907	GL
2	32	0.006	0.003	−0.454	0.033	−0.007	0.003	0.497	0.088	GL
3	32	0.008	0.004	−0.424	0.167	−0.010	0.003	0.473	0.389	GL
4	32	0.007	0.005	−0.333	0.021	−0.009	0.004	0.403	0.038	GL
5	32	0.017	0.014	−0.455	0.014	−0.023	0.012	0.498	0.039	GL
6	32	0.027	0.019	−0.161	0.133	−0.035	0.014	0.278	0.109	GEV
7	32	0.019	0.010	−0.255	0.478	−0.024	0.008	0.345	0.481	GL
8	32	0.012	0.004	−0.326	0.107	−0.014	0.003	0.397	0.163	GL
9	32	0.026	0.018	−0.001	0.008	−0.033	0.012	0.171	0.013	GL
10	35	0.028	0.014	−0.111	0.483	−0.033	0.010	0.243	0.349	GEV

Note: This table includes the PWM parameter estimates and the Anderson–Darling goodness of fit test p-values for the GEV and GL distributions fitted to the monthly minima divided into 2, 4, and 10 sub-periods over the period 1976–2001. N denotes the number of observations, κ, α, β denote the shape, scale, and location parameters, respectively and p-value is the p-value of the Anderson–Darling test statistic.

Table 5. PWM parameter estimates and goodness of fit test for the fitted GEV and GL to the quarterly minima of the ASE index for 1, 2, and 4 sub-periods for the period 1976–2001.

Periods (n)	N	GEV estimates				GL estimates				Better fit
		β	α	κ	p-value	β	α	κ	p-value	
$n = 1$										
1	107	0.022	0.017	−0.254	0.000	−0.029	0.013	0.344	0.002	GL
$n = 2$										
1	54	0.014	0.009	−0.529	0.163	−0.018	0.008	0.559	0.222	GL
2	53	0.036	0.023	0.064	0.004	−0.044	0.014	0.130	0.013	GL
$n = 4$										
1	27	0.011	0.005	−0.520	0.016	−0.014	0.005	0.551	0.057	GL
2	27	0.018	0.012	−0.485	0.095	−0.023	0.010	0.522	0.189	GL
3	27	0.034	0.021	−0.036	0.156	−0.043	0.014	0.193	0.123	GEV
4	26	0.038	0.024	0.197	0.019	−0.046	0.014	0.049	0.022	GL

Note: This table includes the PWM parameter estimates and the Anderson–Darling goodness of fit test p-values for the GEV and GL distributions fitted to the quarterly minima divided into 2 and 4 sub-periods over the period 1976–2001. N denotes the number of observations, κ, α, β denote the shape, scale, and location parameters, respectively and p-value is the p-value of the Anderson–Darling test statistic.

Table 6.   PWM parameters estimates and goodness of fit test for the fitted GEV and GL to the monthly maxima of the ASE index for 1, 2, 4, and 10 sub-periods for the period 1976–2001.

Periods (n)	N	GEV estimates				GL estimates				Better fit
		β	α	κ	p-value	β	α	κ	p-value	
$n = 1$										
1	323	0.015	0.014	-0.237	0.000	0.021	0.010	-0.332	0.001	GEV
$n = 2$										
1	162	0.008	0.007	-0.481	0.123	0.011	0.006	-0.519	0.099	GEV
2	161	0.026	0.016	-0.081	0.010	0.032	0.011	-0.223	0.016	GEV
$n = 4$										
1	80	0.006	0.004	-0.476	0.176	0.008	0.004	-0.515	0.358	GL
2	80	0.011	0.009	-0.447	0.532	0.015	0.008	-0.492	0.441	GEV
3	80	0.024	0.015	-0.203	0.049	0.030	0.011	-0.308	0.053	GEV
4	83	0.027	0.016	0.084	0.066	0.033	0.010	-0.117	0.025	GEV
$n = 10$										
1	32	0.009	0.006	-0.369	0.102	0.011	0.005	-0.430	0.136	GL
2	32	0.005	0.003	-0.491	0.368	0.006	0.003	-0.527	0.626	GL
3	32	0.006	0.004	-0.511	0.338	0.007	0.004	-0.543	0.432	GL
4	32	0.008	0.005	-0.269	0.725	0.010	0.004	-0.355	0.910	GL
5	32	0.022	0.014	-0.427	0.740	0.028	0.012	-0.476	0.887	GL
6	32	0.036	0.024	-0.061	0.668	0.045	0.017	-0.210	0.759	GL
7	32	0.023	0.012	0.028	0.174	0.028	0.008	-0.152	0.124	GEV
8	32	0.014	0.006	-0.193	0.107	0.017	0.004	-0.300	0.217	GL
9	32	0.032	0.016	0.100	0.509	0.038	0.010	-0.107	0.366	GEV
10	35	0.033	0.016	0.165	0.462	0.039	0.009	-0.068	0.205	GEV

Note: This table includes the PWM parameter estimates and the Anderson–Darling goodness of fit test p-values for the GEV and GL distributions fitted to the monthly maxima divided into 2, 4, and 10 sub-periods over the period 1976–2001. N denotes the number of observations, κ, α, β denote the shape, scale, and location parameters, respectively and p-value is the p-value of the Anderson–Darling test statistic.

Table 7. PWM parameters estimates and goodness of fit test for the fitted GEV and GL to the quarterly maxima of the ASE index for 1, 2, and 4 sub-periods for the period 1976–2001.

Periods (n)	N	GEV estimates				GL estimates				Better fit
		β	α	κ	p-value	β	α	κ	p-value	
$n = 1$										
1	107	0.025	0.020	−0.172	0.012	0.033	0.014	−0.285	0.027	GEV
$n = 2$										
1	54	0.015	0.012	−0.426	0.179	0.020	0.010	−0.475	0.206	GL
2	53	0.039	0.021	−0.004	0.426	0.047	0.014	−0.172	0.635	GL
$n = 4$										
1	27	0.012	0.008	−0.437	0.022	0.016	0.007	−0.483	0.053	GL
2	27	0.020	0.015	−0.411	0.390	0.026	0.012	−0.463	0.706	GL
3	27	0.039	0.023	−0.108	0.511	0.048	0.016	−0.241	0.731	GL
4	26	0.042	0.020	0.348	0.117	0.049	0.011	0.035	0.059	GEV

Note: This table includes the PWM parameter estimates and the Anderson–Darling goodness of fit test p-values for the GEV and GL distributions fitted to the quarterly minima divided into 2 and 4 sub-periods over the period 1976–2001. N denotes the number of observations, κ, α, β denote the shape, scale, and location parameters, respectively and p-value is the p-value of the Anderson–Darling test statistic.

test p-value. Finally, in the case of four sub-periods the GL performed better than the GEV in 3 of them. Overall, it is the GL that describes consistently better the empirical data over different sub-periods and selection intervals.

The monthly and quarterly maxima of the ASE index were also been fitted by the GEV and GL distributions and the results are presented in Tables 6 and 7, respectively. Similar to the case of monthly and quarterly minima, the results provided further support to the ability of the GL distribution to fit adequately the extreme daily share returns in the ASE. For example, when monthly maxima divided into 10 sub-periods were fitted the GL fitted 7 sub-periods better than the GEV, although both distributions fitted adequately the data in all sub-periods. The same pattern appeared in the case of quarterly maxima divided into 4 sub-periods with the GL fitting better than the GEV in 3 sub-periods. In addition, the parameters appeared to behave in a similar fashion as in the case of the minima. The scale and location were more volatile during the second half of the whole period while the shape parameter exhibited a tendency to decrease over time from large to small values, in absolute terms, for both distributions. Overall, it is again found that the GL distribution provides a consistently better fit to the ASE index extreme maxima over the period 1976–2001.

Conclusion

This chapter employed innovative EVT methods in order to characterise the asymptotic distribution of the ASE extreme minima and maxima over the period 1976–2001. For this reason, prices from 1976 to 1988 were manually collected from the ASE and combined with prices from 1988 to 2001 collected from electronic sources. Weekly, monthly, and quarterly minima and maxima were then collected as the minimum and maximum daily returns over non-overlapping periods of certain length. A set of probability distributions comprising the GEV and GL was then considered, L-moment ratio diagrams were used as an initial screening of the empirical data, the PWM method was used to estimate the parameters of the most likely distributions to fit the extremes and the AD goodness of fit test was used to assess the adequacy of fit. These EVT techniques can be useful to those interested in risk management since they comprise an additional toolbox for the analysis of extreme stock price movements and the estimation of the associated risk.

In terms of empirical results, it was found that the GL distribution provides adequate descriptions of the ASE index extreme minima and maxima for the period 1976–2001. This finding offers greater support to a limited number of studies (Gettinby *et al.*, 2004; Tolikas *et al.*, 2007) which have also found GL distribution to fit adequately financial extremes. Modelling adequately the tails of financial returns distributions can have important implications for risk management because this is where the really catastrophic events are located. The accurate estimation of their associated probabilities can therefore, lead to more accurate and helpful risk management tools. For example, research has shown that the use of EVT methods in VaR estimation can lead to more accurate estimates of the probabilities of big losses (see, for example, Tolikas *et al.*, 2007; Longin, 2000).

Additionally, the behaviour of the empirical distributions of both the minima and maxima extremes appeared to be time-varying with a tendency to become less fat-tailed over time. These results can be of particular importance to domestic and international investors as well as financial regulators, since less fat-tailed distributions of extremes means that the probabilities of extremes occurring are decreasing and that could lead to increasing confidence amongst market participants and regulators. The latter can have practical implications for portfolio managers with respect to entering or exiting the Greek stock market.

Acknowledgment

Financial support received from the Economic and Social Research Council (ESRC) is greatly acknowledged.

Appendix A

The GEV and GL are three parameter distributions which have the following CDFs, quantile functions, and parameter estimates. The parameters κ, α, and β are called shape, scale, and location, respectively.

Generalised extreme value (GEV)	Generalised logistic (GL)
Cumulative distribution function (CDF)	
$F(x) = e^{-e^{-y}}$	$F(x) = 1/(1 + e^{-y})$
Quantile function	
$X(F) = \begin{cases} \beta + \alpha\{1 - (-\log F)^{\kappa}\}/\kappa, & \kappa \neq 0 \\ \beta - \alpha\log(-\log F), & \kappa = 0 \end{cases}$	$X(F) = \begin{cases} \beta + \alpha[1-\{(1 - F)/F\}^{\kappa}]/\kappa, & \kappa \neq 0 \\ \beta - \alpha\log\{(1 - F)/F\}, & \kappa = 0 \end{cases}$
Parameter estimates	
$\kappa = 7.8590c + 2.9554c^2$	$\kappa = -\tau_3$
where $c = \dfrac{(2\beta_1 - \beta_0)}{(3\beta_2 - \beta_0)} - \dfrac{\ln 2}{\ln 3}$	
$\alpha = \dfrac{\lambda_2 \kappa}{(1 - 2^{-\kappa})\Gamma(1 + \kappa)}$	$\alpha = \dfrac{\lambda_2}{\Gamma(1 - \kappa)\Gamma(1 + \kappa)}$
$\beta = \lambda_1 - \dfrac{\alpha}{\kappa}\{1 - \Gamma(1 + \kappa)\}$	$\beta = \lambda_1 - \dfrac{\alpha}{\kappa}\{1 - \Gamma(1 - \kappa)\Gamma(1 + \kappa)\}$

References

Anderson, TW and DA Darling (1954). A test for goodness of fit. *The American Statistical Association*, 49, 765–769.

Aparicio, FM and J Estrada (2001). Empirical distributions of stock returns: European securities markets, 1990–95. *European Journal of Finance*, 7(1), 1–21.

Basle Committee on Banking Supervision (1996). *Amendment to the Capital Accord to Incorporate Market Risks*. Basle, Switzerland: Bank for International Settlements.

Coles, S and MJ Dixon (1999). Likelihood-based inference for extreme value models. *Extremes*, 2(1), 5–23.

Cotter, J (2001). Margin exceedences for European stock index futures using extreme value theory. *Journal of Banking and Finance*, 25, 1475–1502.

Cunnane, C (1985). Factors effecting choice of distribution for flood series. *Hydrologic Science Journal*, 30(1), 23–36.

d'Agostino, RB and MA Stephens (1986). *Goodness of Fit Techniques*. New York: Marcel Dekker.

de Haan, L, IS Resnick, H Roótzen and CG de Vries (1989). Extremal behaviour of solutions to a stochastic difference equation with applications to ARCH process. *Stochastic Processes and their Applications*, 32, 213–224.

Embrechts, P, S Resnick and G Samorodnitsky (1998). Living on the edge. *Risk*, 11(1), 96–100.

Embrechts, P, C Kluppelberg and T Mikosh (1997). *Modelling Extremal Events*. Berlin: Springer-Verlag.

Gettinby, GD, CD Sinclair, DM Power and RA Brown (2004). An analysis of the distribution of extremes share returns in the UK from 1975 to 2000. *Journal of Business Finance and Accounting*, 31(5–6), 607–645.

Greenwood, JA, JM Landwehr, NC Matalas and JR Wallis (1979). Probability weighted moments: Definition and relation to parameters of several distributions expressable in inverse form. *Water Resources Research*, 15, 1049–1054.

Hosking, JRM and Wallis, JR (1997). *Regional Frequency Analysis: An Approach Based on L-moments*. Cambridge: Cambridge University Press.

Hosking, JRM (1990). L-moments: Analysis and estimation of distributions using linear combinations of order statistics. *Journal of the Royal Statistical Society, Series B*, 52, 105–124.

Hosking, JRM (1986). The theory of probability weighted moments. *IBM T.J. Watson Research Centre* (#54860), pp. 1–160.

Hosking, JRM, JR Wallis and EF Wood (1985). Estimation of the generalised extreme-value distribution by the method of probability-weighted moments. *Technometrics*, 27(3), 251–261.

Jorion, P (2000). *Value-at-Risk: The New Benchmark for Controlling Market Risk*. Chicago: McGraw-Hill.

Landwehr, JM, NC Matalas and JR Wallis (1979). Probability weighted moments compared with some traditional techniques in estimating Gumbel parameters and quantiles. *Water Resources Research*, 15, 1055–1064.

Longin, FM (2000). From value at risk to stress testing: The extreme value approach. *Journal of Banking and Finance*, 24, 1097–1130.

Longin, FM (1996). The asymptotic distribution of extreme stock market returns. *Journal of Business*, 69(3), 383–408.

McNeil, A and R Frey (2000). Estimation of tail-related risk measures for heteroscedastic financial time series: An extreme value approach. *Journal of Empirical Finance*, 7, 271–300.

McNeil, AJ (1999). *Extreme Value Theory for Risk Managers*. Internal Modelling and CAD II. London: Risk Books.

Pandey, MD, PHAJM Van Gelder and JK Vrijling (2001). Assessment of L-kurtosis criterion for quantile estimation. *Journal of Hydrologic Engineering*, 6(4), 284–292.

Peel, MC, QJ Wang, RM Vogel and TA McMahon (2001). The utility of L-moments ratio diagrams for selecting a regional probability distribution. *Hydrological Sciences*, 46(1), 147–155.

Royston, P (1992). Which measures of skewness and kurtosis are best? *Statistics in Medicine*, 11, 333–343.

Sankarasubramanian, A and K Srinivasan (1999). Investigation and comparison of sampling properties of L-moments and conventional moments. *Journal of Hydrology*, 218, 13–34.

Stephens, MA (1976). Asymptotic results for goodness-of-fit statistics with unknown parameters. *Annals of Statistics*, 4(2), 357–369.

Tolikas, K, A Koulakiotis and RA Brown (2007). Extreme risk and value-at-risk in the German stock market. To appear in *European Journal of Finance*, 13(4), 373–395.

3

NAÏVE BAYES AS A MEANS OF CONSTRUCTING APPLICATION SCORECARDS

Anthony C. Antonakis and Michael E. Sfakianakis*

University of Piraeus, Greece

This study examines the effectiveness of the Naïve Bayes Rule relative to that of five other popular algorithms in constructing scorecards that correctly discriminate between good-risk and bad-risk credit applicants. Scorecard performance is assessed on a real-world data sample by both the percentage of correctly classified cases and the more relevant criterion of bad rate among accepts. Naive Bayes is found to produce the worst-performing scorecard under both measures used.

Keywords: Retail banking; credit risk; application scoring; application scorecard; Naïve Bayes.

1. Introduction

The practice of *application scoring* involves the development of a special type of quantitative models (i.e., *application scorecards*) for predicting the future transactional behaviour of any particular credit applicant. Each prospective borrower is assigned to one of two possible behavioural classes: the applicants who are likely to repay their loans (i.e., the good risks) and are, therefore, accepted or the applicants who are likely to default (i.e., the bad risks) and are, therefore, rejected.

---

*Corresponding author.

Scorecards are constructed inductively from a sample of past applicants with known class memberships. A learning algorithm is typically applied to this *training set* for identifying a relationship between an applicant's *characteristics* (demographic, economic, and other variables) and his/her exhibited behaviour. After that, given the characteristics of each new applicant, his/her likely future behaviour can easily be predicted.

One such algorithm that is frequently used in supervised classification problems like the one described above is the *Naïve Bayes Rule* (NBR). Despite its usually unrealistic assumption of class conditionally independent predictors, many studies (see the Literature Review section) report NBR to outperform more sophisticated alternatives in constructing accurate classification rules. However, it has not been at the centre of academic research in the field of application scoring.

The purpose of this study is to benchmark NBR against five other learning algorithms as a method for constructing accurate application scorecards. Scorecard performance is assessed on real-world data by both the popular criterion of the percentage of correctly classified cases (PCC) and the more relevant (Hand and Kelly, 2002; Hand, 2005) criterion of the bad rate among accepts (BRA).

To the best of our knowledge, the only previous study that used BRA to evaluate the performance of NBR in the context of application scoring was that of Antonakis and Sfakianakis (2005). The study presented here builds upon this last study, by including comparisons with three more algorithms and conducting a more thorough analysis of the experimental results.

The rest of this chapter is organised as follows. The following section briefly reviews literature on the use of NBR in supervised classification and application scoring. The subsequent section explains how each of the algorithms investigated here can be used for scorecard construction. The next section discusses the use of PCC and BRA as performance criteria. The following two sections describe the methodology and present the experimental results, respectively. The final section concludes.

2. Literature Review

Many studies involve the use of NBR as a tool for constructing classification rules. This section aims to review a selection of these studies, particularly those that are crucial for the analysis that follows (for a comprehensive review of NBR-related studies, see Hand and Yu, 2001). Despite its simplistic nature, these studies often show that NBR can be more effective than sophisticated approaches for supervised classification tasks.

Kohavi (1996) used data from many different domains to demonstrate that the accuracy of NBR does not scale up well as sample size increases and introduced a decision tree hybrid that outperforms both constituents in large data sets.

Domingos and Pazzani (1997) conducted a large-scale study as well. They found NBR to outperform three "state-of-the-art" learning algorithms, even in situations that allowed for some dependence and went on to show that NBR can be optimal for a wider range of situations than was previously thought.

Friedman *et al.* (1997) similarly found NBR to outperform unrestricted Bayesian networks on a large sample of benchmark data sets. They then proposed a much more limited extension that was indeed more accurate than NBR on the same data sets. Hand and Yu (2001) examined empirical and theoretical evidence for the effectiveness of NBR and identified reasons for its surprisingly good performance. While NBR has received much attention in other problem areas, few related studies have been published in the context of application scoring.

Hand and Adams (2000) were probably the first to apply NBR in this context. They compared NBR with logistic regression using several performance criteria. They found the former to perform worse than the latter, except from the case of an artificial data set where NBR was expected to be optimal.

Baesens *et al.* (2002) benchmarked NBR against one decision tree and two Bayesian network classifiers. The relative performance rankings of methods varied, depending on the performance criterion used (area under the ROC curve, PCC).

Finally, Antonakis and Sfakianakis (2005) contrasted NBR to linear discriminant analysis and logistic regression. They found NBR to perform worse than the other two methods under both PCC and BRA.

It appears that application scoring studies are not as favorable for NBR as studies in other domains are. They also seem to indicate that selection of different performance criteria may lead to different conclusions regarding its predictive ability. This probably justifies the use of two different criteria (PCC and BRA) for comparison purposes. Before the analysis is conducted, it is necessary to see how NBR and other algorithms can be applied for scorecard construction.

3. Scorecard Construction

Scorecards estimate the probability p_G that an applicant is a good risk. If p_G is found to be greater than a suitably chosen threshold (i.e., the *cut-off point*), then the applicant is classified as a good risk and is accepted, otherwise the applicant is classified as a bad risk and is rejected. This section addresses the estimation of p_G, while the next one attends to the selection of the cut-off point. More information on the methods described here is given by Thomas (2000), Hand (2001), and Antonakis and Sfakianakis (2006).

Application scorecards estimate p_G as a function of the applicant's characteristics. Characteristics can be either categorical (e.g., marital status, residential status, etc.) or quantitative (e.g., age, income, etc.). A standard process is to split quantitative characteristics into categories and treat them as categorical (Thomas, 2000). Then, each category is treated as a dummy variable and is assigned a risk-weighted coefficient via a learning algorithm.

Let D be the total number of dummy variables, x_k, w_k be the corresponding risk-weighted coefficients and $j = 0, 1$ be the indicators for the bad and the good risk class, respectively. Then *Linear Discriminant Analysis* (LDA) calculates the discriminant score:

$$Z = \sum_{k=1}^{D} x_k w_k \tag{1}$$

where vector w is chosen to maximise the between-group variance relative to the within-group variance (Desai *et al.*, 1996), and estimates the posterior probability $p_G = P(1|Z)$ as:

$$p_G = \frac{P(Z|1)P(1)}{\left(\sum_{j=0}^{1} P(Z|j)P(j) \right)} \tag{2}$$

On the other hand, both NBR and *Logistic Regression Analysis* (LRA) assume that:

$$\ln \left(\frac{p_G}{(1 - p_G)} \right) = \sum_{k=1}^{D} x_k w_k \tag{3}$$

While LRA estimates the weights in (3) by maximum likelihood, NBR assumes class conditional independence of characteristics Z_i and defines the weights as

$$w_i = \ln \left(\frac{\widehat{f}_i(z_i|1)}{\widehat{f}_i(z_i|0)} \right) \qquad (4)$$

where the class conditional probabilities $\widehat{f}_i(z_i|j)$, are estimated according to Hand and Adams (2000) and Hand (2001).

Classification Trees (CT) (Breiman *et al.*, 1984) partition the vector space of applicant characteristics into nonoverlapping subspaces (*cells*), each one being as homogeneous as possible within itself and as different as possible from the others regarding risk. Choosing a certain characteristic and a particular split of its values in a way that best satisfies the above condition, CT initially partition the whole space into two cells. CT then repeat this process for each resulting cell until they reach a *terminal cell*, i.e., a cell that is not reasonable to split anymore either because it is too small to do so or because it cannot be split into even more risk-pure cells. These models estimate the probability p_G that an applicant in a terminal cell is a good risk by the relative proportion of good risk applicants in this cell (Hand, 2001).

The most popular form of *Neural Networks* (NN) (Lee *et al.*, 2002; Chen and Huang, 2003) consists of processing elements (i.e., *neurons*) organised in layers. There is always one input and one output layer and a number of hidden layers (usually one) in between. Each non-input layer neuron receives numerical inputs from every neuron in the previous layer and delivers a transformation of the weighted sum of these inputs as output to every neuron in the next layer.

Input-layer neurons represent applicant characteristics. There is typically a single output-layer neuron that is set to estimate p_G. Weights are initially set to randomly chosen numbers and the difference between p_G and the known class indicator is calculated for all training observations. The mean squared error is then propagated backwards through the network in proportion to the contribution made to it by each weight and the weights are adjusted accordingly to reduce this error. By repeating this process until a stopping criterion is met, the correct NN architecture is identified.

Application scorecards try to predict an applicant's future behaviour by comparing his/her profile with that of similar past applicants. The *k-Nearest Neighbor* (*k*-NN) approach (Henley and Hand, 1996) defines a metric in the vector space of applicant characteristics and measures similarity by the corresponding distance. This method maps each applicant to a point in this space and estimates p_G by the proportion of good risks among the k nearest (i.e., most similar) points in the training set.

Modern, sophisticated classifiers, such as NN, k-NN, and CT, are more capable of modelling the "smaller" features of the underlying distributions than traditional, simple techniques, such as NBR, LDA and LRA. Of course, this increased flexibility of sophisticated classifiers may well be an advantage. However, as Hand (2006) argues, in practice there are many *sources of uncertainty* (change of distributions over time, sample selectivity bias, arbitrariness in the class definitions, etc.) that are generally not considered in the classical supervised classification paradigm and that may negatively affect sophisticated approaches to a larger extent than the simple methods, which model the "grosser" features of the distributions. Hand (2006) suggests that the small improvements in performance that are often attributed to sophisticated classifiers may well be swamped by these sources of uncertainty and not translate into real advantages in practice.

This section examined how application scorecards can be used to estimate probabilities of repayment. Before going on, it is necessary to understand how these estimates can be used to accept/reject credit applicants. This has to do with selecting the suitable cut-off probability and scorecard performance measure.

4. Scorecard Performance Measures

From the previous section we know that if an applicant has repayment probability p_G greater than a suitably chosen cut-off point t, then the applicant is accepted; otherwise he/she is rejected. The question then is how to choose t.

Since the relative severity of misclassification costs is often hard to determine exactly (Adams and Hand, 1999), a cut-off point of $t = 0.5$ is typically used and scorecard performance is assessed on the basis of the *percentage of correctly classified cases* (PCC). However, this implicitly assumes equal misclassification costs. This may be a valid assumption to make for other classification problems but it is probably not for application scoring, because misclassifying a bad applicant as good (Type II error) is a more serious mistake than the opposite (Type I error). Another weakness of choosing t on the basis of some cost-weighted loss measure, such as PCC, is that one cannot calculate such a cost-weighted measure because one needs to take into account the applicants whom the lender will reject and, thus, will never find out their true behavioural class, be it good or bad (Hand, 2005).

For these reasons, Hand and Kelly (2002) and Hand (2005) recommend ranking applicants according to risk and selecting the cut-off point (i.e., the *accept rate*) on the basis of the corresponding *bad rate among those accepted* (BRA). Thus, when lenders want to assess the predictive ability of a scorecard, they must first decide on a desirable accept rate (or range of accept rates) and then examine the corresponding bad rate(s) of the scorecard.

To see if different conclusions can be drawn on the basis of different criteria, both PCC and BRA are used to assess the relative performance of scorecards constructed by the six algorithms investigated in this study.

5. Methodology

For the purposes of this study, a real-world data set from a major Greek bank was used. This data set consisted of 5340 past applicants for a consumer credit product to whom credit had been extended. Of these applicants, 4885 were good risks and 455 were bad risks. The relative proportion of behavioural classes reflects the true relative proportion in the records of the bank for the time period during which the data were collected. Of the total number of cases, 80% were used as the training set and the remaining 20% as the test set.

For each applicant the values of 15 characteristics and his/her class indicator were available. For reasons of data confidentiality, the exact nature of characteristics cannot be disclosed. Quantitative characteristics were discretised according to homogeneity of risk, as in Thomas (2000) and Yobas *et al.* (2000), so that all characteristics were grouped into categories. Of these 15 categorical characteristics, 11 exhibited an information value of at least 0.1, a value above which characteristics are considered to be useful in differentiating good from bad risks (Henley and Hand, 1996), and were thus selected for inclusion in the scorecards. Table 1 provides some information on these 11 characteristics. The four characteristics that were not selected for inclusion in the analysis were binary categorical variables with information values of 0.05, 0.04, 0.03, and 0.02.

In the case of NBR, the 11 categorical characteristics that passed the selection process were used as predictors, following the exact specifications by Hand and Adams (2000) and Hand (2001). For all other methods, the same 11 categorical characteristics were typically split into dummy variables representing categories. Initially there were a total of 38 dummy variables (see Table 1). For each of the 11 characteristics, one of the resulting dummy variables (the one with the lowest information value) was excluded from the

Table 1.   Applicant characteristics.

Characteristic	Original type	Categories	Information value	Dummy variables
C1	Categorical	3	1.43	2
C2	Continuous	4	0.61	3
C3	Continuous	4	0.56	3
C4	Continuous	3	0.39	2
C5	Categorical	2	0.35	1
C6	Categorical	3	0.32	2
C7	Categorical	2	0.25	1
C8	Continuous	4	0.24	3
C9	Continuous	3	0.17	2
C10	Continuous	4	0.16	3
C11	Categorical	6	0.16	5
Total		38	—	27

analysis to avoid computational problems arising from the use of redundant variables, such as perfect collinearity in the case of LDA and LRA. This left us with $38 - 11 = 27$ dummy variables to include in the analysis.

The NBR, LDA, and LRA models were specified as in the scorecard construction section. For NN the number of epochs was set to 45, learning rate to 0.1, and momentum to 0.8 (Chen and Huang, 2003). Distance in the space of applicant characteristics for k-NN was measured by the Euclidean metric, even though alternative approaches can also be used (Hand and Henley, 1996). Other learning parameters for NN, k-NN, and CT were chosen through trial-and-error on the test set. Values of 16–25 for number of hidden layer neurons, 1–10 for k, and $0.1\%, 0.2\%, \ldots, 1.0\%$ of the training set for terminal cell size were tested, respectively, so that for NN, k-NN, and CT the same number (ten) of alternative model structures was tested. All routines were performed using XLMiner®, version 3.0.

6. Findings

Table 2 reports PCC for the scorecards constructed by each of the six algorithms and is supplemented with 95% confidence intervals. Total PCC is broken down into the percentage of correctly classified good risks and the percentage of correctly classified bad risks.

Results in Table 2 suggest that, in terms of total PCC, k-NN perform best and that NBR performs worst. One should note, however, that the differences in total PCC between the methods are small. In fact, the difference between the apparently best (i.e., k-NN) and the apparently worst (i.e., NBR) method

Table 2. Percentage of correctly classified cases (PCC): 95% confidence intervals.

Algorithm	Total	Good	Bad
k-NN	94.8 ± 1.3	98.2 ± 0.8	58.2 ± 10.1
NN	94.5 ± 1.4	97.0 ± 1.1	67.0 ± 9.7
CT	93.8 ± 1.4	98.1 ± 0.9	48.4 ± 10.3
LRA	93.1 ± 1.5	97.1 ± 1.1	49.5 ± 10.3
LDA	92.7 ± 1.6	96.7 ± 1.1	49.5 ± 10.3
NBR	91.0 ± 1.7	94.2 ± 1.5	57.1 ± 10.2

is within two standard deviations. This means that the differences in total PCC are not significant.

Results in Table 2 also illustrate why PCC (i.e., a cut-off of 0.5) is an inappropriate criterion for application scoring. Only just over a half of the bad risks are correctly classified. Since Type II error is more serious than Type I error (Lee *et al.*, 2002), a scorecard that is better in terms of the real problem would result from misclassifying fewer bad risks, even if this scorecard had a smaller PCC.

Given that NBR exhibits a low Type II error (relative to most of the other algorithms), perhaps if the cut-off point were adjusted so that the methods misclassified the same proportion of bad risks, NBR would correctly classify more good risks and look better than PCC implies. To test if the above is true, ROC curves were plotted as in Figure 1.

ROC curves (Hand and Henley, 1997) plot the percentage of good risks that are above a certain cut-off point against the percentage of bad risks that are above the same cut-off point. Lower percentages of accepted bad risks correspond to higher cut-off point values and vice versa. In this sense, ROC curves provide a global view of how scorecards compare under different cut-off point values. An ideal scorecard in such a plot would follow the *Y*-axis from point (0,0) to point (0,100) and then the *X*-axis from point (0,100) to point (100,100).

Figure 1 shows the ROC curves for NN (with 20 neurons in the hidden layer), *k*-NN (with *k* = 7), LRA, and NBR. To achieve better visualisation, the ROC curves for CT and LDA are not shown. For nearly all possible cut-off point values NN performs best, followed by LRA and *k*-NN. Once again, NBR is found to perform poorly, with its ROC curve being dominated by the curves of the other methods over nearly all possible values (NBR is better than *k*-NN for very high cut-off point values). Of the methods not depicted in Fig. 1, CT (with terminal cell size of 0.3% of the training set) perform comparably to LRA and *k*-NN, while LDA is only better than NBR.

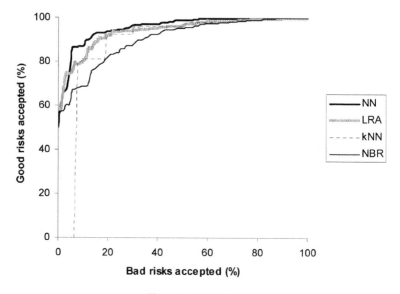

Figure 1.   ROC curves.

In practice, lenders would especially care about how scorecards perform over a particular range of cut-off points that are more relevant for the problem at hand (Adams and Hand, 1999). To shed more light upon this matter, BRA was examined for a range (70–90%) of reasonable accept rates as in Table 3. Lower values correspond to lower proportions of bad risks among those accepted, hence they are associated with better scorecards. Results for NN, k-NN, and CT correspond to the model structures that perform best over the entire 70–90% range, that is 20 neurons in the hidden layer for NN, $k = 7$ for k-NN and terminal cell size of 0.3% of the training set for CT.

Table 3.   Bad rate (%) among accepts (BRA) for various accept rates.

	Accept Rate (%)				
Algorithm	70	75	80	85	90
NN	0.7	0.6	0.8	1.4	2.8
k-NN	0.9	1.1	2.1	2.0	2.9
CT	1.1	1.2	1.9	1.9	3.1
LRA	0.8	1.2	1.5	2.0	3.4
LDA	0.8	1.2	1.6	2.5	3.5
NBR	1.6	2.1	2.7	3.2	4.2

Table 3, again, suggests that NN perform best and that NBR performs worst. Results under BRA are very important, because, as it has already been stated, BRA is arguably the most suitable criterion for application scoring.

It is interesting that NBR is found to perform poorly under all criteria used. This observation makes it necessary to examine if this finding can be attributed to any particular properties of the data. An obvious starting point is to test if the class conditional independence assumption of NBR is violated. Since the 11 raw categorical characteristics were used as predictors in the case of NBR, dependence given the class C was computed for all characteristic pairs A_m and A_n, excluding pairings of a characteristic with itself, using measure (Wan and Wong, 1989; Kononenko, 1991; Domingos and Pazzani, 1997):

$$D(A_m, A_n|C) = H(A_m|C) + H(A_n|C) - H(A_mA_n|C) \qquad (5)$$

where A_mA_n is the Cartesian product of A_m and A_n, and for all classes i and characteristic values k:

$$H(A_j|C) = \sum_i P(C_i) \sum_k -P(C_i \wedge A_j = u_{jk}) \log_2 P(C_i \wedge A_j = u_{jk}) \qquad (6)$$

Measure D is zero when A_m and A_n are completely independent given C, and increases with their degree of dependence, with the maximum occurring when the class and one characteristic completely determine the other.

Table 4 summarises the results. The first row reports the maximum value of D observed. The second row reports the percentage of all characteristics that had a degree of dependence with some other characteristic of at least 0.2, a value commonly used as a threshold above which characteristics are considered to be significantly dependent (Domingos and Pazzani, 1997). The third and the fourth row report the average and the median value of D.

Comparing the above results with those of Table 3 of Domingos and Pazzani (1997), it appears that many (seven out of eleven) of the applicant characteristics exhibit a significant degree of dependence with some other characteristic. Judging also from the average and the median value of D,

Table 4. Empirical measures of characteristic dependence.

Max. D	0.484
$\%D > 0.2$	63.6
Avg. D	0.169
Med. D	0.143

there is definitely a considerable degree of dependence in the data. Even though NBR can be optimal in situations that allow for some degree of dependence, as Domingos and Pazzani (1997) suggest, violation of the independence assumption, which is evident in the data used in this study, may be one reason for the low predictive ability exhibited here by NBR.

Another possible reason for the poor performance of NBR relative to the other five highly parameterised algorithms may be the large sample size. We know that because of their low variance (Domingos and Pazzani, 1997; Hand and Yu, 2001), it is possible for the predictive accuracy of NBR-built classification rules to asymptote earlier than that of more sophisticated alternatives (Kohavi, 1996). This appears to be exactly the case not only in this study, but also in the study of Hand and Adams (2000) that also produced results unfavourable to NBR (Examples 1 and 3).

7. Conclusion

As previous studies (Domingos and Pazzani, 1997; Friedman *et al.*, 1997; Hand and Yu, 2001) demonstrate, NBR can be highly effective in supervised classification tasks. However, results on real-world application scoring data in this study indicate that NBR performs worse than five other alternatives as a method for constructing scorecards that correctly classify consumer credit applicants as good or bad risks.

There appear to be good reasons why application scoring data may be expected to produce results unfavourable to NBR. First of all, it is reasonable to assume that the significant degree of dependence exhibited in this study is inherent in this type of data. One can easily think for example of pairs of typical application scoring characteristics, such as marital status and number of children or age and years of professional experience, that are expected to be highly dependent. This clearly violates the independence assumption of NBR and may cause this rule to perform poorly.

It is also possible for the classification accuracy of NBR to asymptote earlier than that of more flexible models, such as NN, k-NN, or CT (Kohavi, 1996). This means that as the sample size increases, so it becomes possible to fit these more flexible models, which tend to pick up small real aspects of the data (such as the dependence structure) that simple approaches (like NBR) cannot easily identify. This may be a disadvantage for NBR in the domain of application scoring, where sample sizes are typically in the thousands, even though the simplicity and speed of calculations of NBR could be particularly useful for very large samples.

However, as Hand (2006) argues, one should note that these more flexible models (in our case NN, k-NN, CT, or even LRA, as a generalisation of NBR) are more vulnerable than NBR to sources of uncertainty (population drift, sample selectivity bias, arbitrariness in the class definitions, etc.) that are generally not considered in the classical supervised classification paradigm, as the case is in this study. This means that in practice (i.e., in the face of the above uncertainties) the improvements in performance that are attributed to these sophisticated classifiers relative to NBR may not translate into real advantages. This may be particularly true in situations where these improvements are small, as the case is with total PCC results in this study.

Another disadvantage (Duin, 1996; Hand, 2006) of these more flexible classifiers relative to NBR is that they have many user-adjustable learning parameters, such as the number of nodes in NN or the metric in k-NN. Given that there is no formal theory to determine the optimal model structure, decisions regarding the choice of appropriate values for these parameters must be taken using experimentation. Therefore, results are sensitive to the selection of these parameters. It is for the reasons described above that Duin (1996) and Hand (2006) argue that comparisons involving these classifiers have limitations in that different people, with different degrees of expertise in using the different classifiers could draw different conclusions. Future researchers may wish to address these issues. Another point to consider for further research arises from the fact that in practice banks often use more complex approaches for the purpose of screening credit applicants than the ones described here. For example, banks may combine CT with LRA (Hand, 2001). Researchers could also include these more complex methods in future comparisons and benchmark NBR against them as well.

References

Adams, NM and DJ Hand (1999). Comparing classifiers when the misallocation costs are uncertain. *Pattern Recognition*, 32, 1139–1147.

Antonakis, A and M Sfakianakis (2005). Knowledge management as a means of achieving organizational excellence: A retail-banking case. *Proceedings of the International Conference on Managing Global Trends and Challenges in a Turbulent Economy*. Chios, Greece: University of the Aegean.

Antonakis, A and M Sfakianakis (2006). Knoweledge management for evaluating borrower creditworthiness as a competitive advantage in the banking sector. In *Knowledge Management and Governing Systems: Proceedings of the 1st National Conference of HSSS*, pp. 758–764. Tripoli, Greece: HSSS.

Baesens, B, M Egmont-Petersen, R Castelo and J Vanthienen (2002). Learning Bayesian network classifiers for credit scoring using Markov Chain Monte Carlo search. In *Proceedings of the 16th International Conference on Pattern Recognition (ICPR'02)*, Vol. 3, pp. 49–52. Quebec City, Quebec: IEEE Computer Society Press.

Breiman L, JH Friedman, RA Olshen and CJ Stone (1984). *Classification and Regression Trees*. Belmont: Wadsworth.

Chen, MC and SH Huang (2003). Credit scoring and rejected instances reassigning through evolutionary computational techniques. *Expert Systems with Applications*, 24, 433–441.

Desai, VS, JN Crook and GA Overstreet (1996). A comparison of neural networks and linear scoring models in the credit union environment. *European Journal of Operational Research*, 95, 24–37.

Domingos, P and M Pazzani (1997). On the optimality of the simple Bayesian classifier under zero-one loss. *Machine Learning*, 29, 103–130.

Duin, RPW (1996). A note on comparing classifiers. *Pattern Recognition Letters*, 17, 529–536.

Friedman, N, D Geiger and M Goldszmidt (1997). Bayesian network classifiers. *Machine Learning*, 29, 131–163.

Hand, DJ (2001). Modelling consumer credit risk. *IMA Journal of Management Mathematics*, 12, 139–155.

Hand, DJ (2005). Good practice in retail credit scorecard assessment. *Journal of the Operational Research Society*, 56, 1109–1117.

Hand, DJ (2006). Classifier technology and the illusion of progress (with discussion). *Statistical Science*, 21, 1–34.

Hand, DJ and NM Adams (2000). Defining attributes for scorecard construction in credit scoring. *Journal of Applied Statistics*, 27, 527–540.

Hand, DJ and WE Henley (1997). Statistical classification methods in consumer credit scoring: A review. *Journal of the Royal Statistical Society, Series A*, 160, 523–541.

Hand, DJ and MG Kelly (2002). Superscorecards. *IMA Journal of Management Mathematics*, 13, 273–281.

Hand, DJ and K Yu (2001). Idiot's Bayes — Not so stupid after all. *International Statistical Review*, 69, 385–398.

Henley, WE and DJ Hand (1996). A k-Nearest-Neighbour classifier for assessing consumer credit risk. *The Statistician*, 45, 77–95.

Kohavi, R (1996). Scaling up the accuracy of Naïve-Bayes classifiers: A decision-tree hybrid. In *Proceedings of the 2nd International Conference on Knowledge Discovery and Data Mining*, pp. 202–207. Portland, OR: AAAI Press.

Kononenko, I (1991). Semi-naïve Bayesian classifier. In *Proceedings of the 6th European Working Session on Learning*, pp. 206–219. Porto, Portugal: Springer-Verlag.

Lee, TS, CC Chiu, CJ Lu and IF Chen (2002). Credit scoring using the hybrid neural discriminant technique. *Expert Systems with Applications*, 23, 245–254.

Thomas, LC (2000). A survey of credit and behavioural scoring: Forecasting financial risk of lending to consumers. *International Journal of Forecasting*, 16, 149–172.

Yobas, MB, JN Crook and P Ross (2000). Credit scoring using neural and evolutionary techniques. *IMA Journal of Mathematics Applied in Business and Industry*, 11, 111–125.

Wan, SJ and SKM Wong (1989). A measure for concept dissimilarity and its applications in machine learning. In *Proceedings of the International Conference on Computing and Information*, pp. 267–273. Toronto, Ontario: North-Holland.

————————— 4 —————————

ON THE BENEFITS OF INDUSTRIAL NETWORK: A NEW APPROACH WITH MARKET SURVEY AND FUZZY STATISTICAL ANALYSIS

Shu-Meei Ho

Chihlee Institute of Technology, Taiwan

Berlin Wu

National Chengchi University, Taiwan

Making the most of the industrial network to reduce management costs and increase competitiveness has gained a lot of attention among enterprises lately. In traditional market research methods, the approach has always been to put the emphasis on the data of a single value without considering the complexity of human thoughts. Thus, it is the purpose of this paper to first define fuzzy mode, fuzzy expect value and fuzzy χ^2 test. Then, a new market survey is proposed to develop a more efficient survey analysis to examine the characteristics of the fuzzy questionnaire and sample material. A comparison between the fuzzy χ^2 *test and traditional* χ^2 test will be carried on at the end.

Keywords: Industrial network; marketing survey; fuzzy statistical analysis.

1. Introduction

Ideally, the function of the industrial network is to support the cooperation among enterprises. The influence is always be mutual. In reality, it either increases cooperation within the alliance, or cause competition among

---

*Corresponding author.

different types of businesses. In other words, the collaboration is originally formed to reduce transaction costs. Nevertheless, the integration may possibly endanger the development of free markets and become monopolised.

Many scholars in different fields have provided a positive perspective on the business industry structure from the industry network point of view. Management scholars believe that the long-term interaction among businesses is the key to successful marketing based on business capital information and resource benefits. Finance and economics scholars, on the other hand, emphasise the influence of transaction costs, i.e., how to reduce transaction uncertainties through industrial network. From the above, it is understandable that small and mid-scale businesses can obtain the economic strength once owned by large-scale organisations and still retain their flexibility through industrial network.

Through the industry network, the business either consequently produces favourable benefits or reduces unfavourable costs or loss toward the organisation (Jarillo, 1988). The existence of a network can not only disperse risks but also allow the business to concentrate on the value-chain that is an essential activity in achieving higher competitiveness. This kind of superiority is especially important in a high-tech and competitive environment.

Recognising the significant heterogeneity and dependence that the industrial network may contribute to a business, recent research in marketing has been directed at the evaluation as well as accommodation of richer related structures. In order to investigate the benefits of a business network, we need to expand the current method of analysis by examining it from a wider, systemic point of view. As traditional statistics reflect the result from a two-valued-logic world, to investigate the population, public opinions or the complexity of a subjective event more accurately, it is suggested that we use fuzzy logic. Fuzzy statistics provides a powerful research tool, especially if we want to know something such as the public ideology on the environmental pollution. Moreover, since Zadeh (1965) developed fuzzy set theory, its applications have been extended to traditional statistical inferences and methods in social sciences, including medical diagnosis or a stock investment system. For example, Ruspini (1991), Tseng and Klein (1992) demonstrated the approximate reasoning econometric methods one after another. Wu and Hsu (2004) developed fuzzy time series model to overcome the bias of stock market.

More and more researchers are focusing on the fuzzy statistical analysis and applications in the social science fields, such as Guariso, Rizzoli and Werthner (1992), who identified the model construction through qualitative simulation; and Wu and Tseng (2002) who used fuzzy regression method of coefficient estimation to analyse Taiwan's economic index. Recently, along with the raise in awareness of intelligent knowledge consciousness and soft computing, many investigators are focusing on the application of fuzzy set in prediciting human thoughts or public polls under the uncertain and incomplete conditions.

2. Network Benefits

Because of the close geographical locations of the industry business groups, lower transportation costs can be achieved. Moreover, communication among those groups will be extended and closer. It is also easier to build trust and maintain long-term partnership. Thus, not only can the efficiency of business production be improved, both transaction costs and operating costs are also lowered.

The goal of forming an industry network can be summarised as follows:

(1) *Maintaining joint cooperation, competitiveness, and stable relationships:* Similar business firms join together to either devise a way of improving the business condition or face competition effectively. Mutual trust is a must for a long-term partnership in order for it to further engage in quality variation or service-level improvement.

(2) *Using adequate e-commerce organisation management:* Through different kinds of network, research and development resources can be exchanged rapidly to adjust to mutual production capacity.

(3) *Grasping new opportunities and reducing risks:* Concrete strategic alliance or transparent network relations may be able to assist the enterprise in reducing possible risks.

(4) *Expanding scale of businesses and improving working efficiency:* Cooperation among small or mid-scale businesses can help to reduce the costs, increase the level of new product research and development for time-to-market opportunities and upgrade the lead time and flexibility of delivery. Purchasing union will be able to display better negotiating strength under the circumstances.

The benefits of industry network system include the following:

(1) *Reducing costs:* Industry networks among enterprises can expand economic areas and achieve network economic interests and thus, reduce transaction costs.

(2) *Dispersing risk:* Uncertainty in production can be cut down due to long-term cooperation. Certain risks can also be reduced based on mutual relationship.

(3) *Obtaining major resources effectively:* After the formation of a business network system, the learning and sharing of knowledge expertise become faster and more effective.

(4) *Improving the competitive status:* Through the allied network, the enterprises unite to develop new products, perform product improvements, and provide overall customer service. That helps in elevating the market competitive status of the enterprise.

3. Fuzzy Statistical Analysis and its Applications in the Market Survey

3.1. *The nature of fuzzy samples*

Traditional statistics deal with single answers or certain range of an answer through sampling survey, but it has difficulty in reflecting people's incomplete and uncertain thoughts. In other words, these processes often ignore the intriguing, complicated, yet sometimes conflicting, human logic and feelings. If people can use the membership function[a] to express the degree of their feelings based on their own understanding, the result will be closer to their real thoughts. For instance, when people process a pollution assessment, they classify the distraction into two categories: pollution and non-pollution. This kind of classification is not realistic, since the pollution is a fuzzy concept (varying in degree) and can hardly be justified by the true-false logic. Therefore, to compute the information based on the fuzzy logic would be more reasonable.

In considering the question related to fuzzy property, we suppose the information itself has uncertainty and fuzzy property. Hence, let's firstly give an easy and precise explanation about fuzzy numbers.

Definition 3.1. Fuzzy number

Let U denote a universal set, $\{A_i\}_{i=1}^{n}$ be a subset of discussion factors on U, and $\Lambda(A_i)$ be a level set of A_i for $i = 1, 2, \ldots, n$. The fuzzy number of a

---

[a]The membership function of a fuzzy set is a generalisation of the indicator function in classical sets. In fuzzy logic, it represents the degree of truth as an extension of valuation. Degrees of truth are often confused with probabilities, although they are conceptually district, because fuzzy truth represents membership in vague defined sets, not likelihood of same event or condition. Membership functions were introduced by Zadeh in the first paper on fuzzy sets (1965).

statement or a term X over U is defined as:

$$\mu_U(X) = \sum_{i=1}^{n} \mu_i(X) I_{A_i}(X) \qquad (3.1)$$

where $\{\mu_i(X), 0 \leq \mu_i(X) \leq 1\}_{i=1}^{n}$ is a set of membership functions for corresponding factor in $\{A_i\}_{i=1}^{n}$, and $I_{A_i}(x) = 1$ if $x \in A_i : I_{A_i}(x) = 0$ if $x \notin A_i$. If the domain of the universal set is continuous, then the fuzzy number can be written as: $\mu_U(X) = \int_{A_i \subseteq A} \mu_i(X) I_{A_i}(X)$.

In social sciences research, the sampling survey is always used to evaluate and understand public opinion on certain issues. The traditional survey forces people to choose one answer from the survey, but it ignores the uncertainty in human thinking. For instance, when people need to choose the answer from the survey which lists five choices including "very satisfactory", "satisfactory", "normal", "unsatisfactory", "very unsatisfactory", the traditional survey becomes quite exclusive.

The advantages of evaluation with fuzzy number include: (i) evaluation process becomes robust and consistent by reducing the degree of subjectivity of the evaluator; (ii) self-potentiality is highlighted by indicating individual distinctions; (iii) The evaluators are provided with an encouraging, stimulating, self-reliant guide that emphasises on individual characteristics. The drawback is that the calculating process will be a little complex than the traditional one.

Traditional statistics deal with single answers or certain range of an answer through sampling survey, and are unable to sufficiently reflect the complex thought of an individual. If people can use the membership function to express the degree of their feelings based on their own choices, the answer presented will be closer to real human thinking. Therefore, to collect information based on the fuzzy mode should be the first step taken. Very often, the information itself is embedded with uncertainty and ambiguity. It is nature for us to propose fuzzy statistics, such as fuzzy mode and fuzzy median, to fit the modern requirement. In this and next section we demonstrate the definitions for fuzzy mode and fuzzy median generalised from the traditional statistics. The discrete case is simpler than the continuous one.

Definition 3.2. Fuzzy mode (data with multiple values)
Let U be the universal set (a discussion domain), $L = \{L_1, L_2, \ldots, L_k\}$ be a set of k-linguistic variables on U, and $\{FS_i, i = 1, 2, \ldots, n\}$ be a sequence of random fuzzy sample on U. For each sample FS_i, assign a linguistic variable L_j a

normalised membership $m_{ij}(\sum_{j=1}^{k} m_{ij} = 1)$, let $S_j = \sum_{i=1}^{n} m_{ij}, j = 1, 2, \ldots, k$. Then, the maximum value of S_j (with respect to L_j) is called the fuzzy mode (FM) of this sample. That is $FM = \{L_j | S_j = \max_{1 \leq i \leq k} S_i\}$.

Definition 3.3. Fuzzy mode (data with interval values)
Let U be the universe set (a discussion domain), $L = \{L_1, L_2, \ldots, L_k\}$ be a set of k-linguistic variables on U, and $\{FS_i = [a_i, b_i], a_i, b_i \in R, i = 1, 2, \ldots, n\}$ be a sequence of random fuzzy sample on U. For each sample FS_i, if there is an interval $[c, d]$ which is covered by certain samples, we denote these samples as a clustering. Let MS is the set of clustering which contains the maximum number of samples, then the fuzzy mode FM is defined as

$$FM = [a, b] = \{\cap[a_i, b_i] | [a_i, b_i] \subset MS\}.$$

If $[a, b]$ does not exist (i.e., $[a, b]$ is an empty set), we say this fuzzy sample does not have fuzzy mode.

3.2. A χ^2-test for fuzzy categorical data

Consider a K-cell multinomial vector $n = \{n_1, n_2, \ldots, n_k\}$ with $\sum_i n_i = n$. The Person chi-squared test ($\chi^2 = \sum_i \sum_j \frac{n_{ij} - e_{ij}}{e_{ij}}$) is a well known statistical test for investigating the significance of the differences between observed data arranged in K classes and the theoretically expected frequencies in the K classes. It is clear that the large discrepancies between the observed data and expected cell counts will result in larger values of χ^2.

However, a somewhat ambiguous question is whether (quantitative) discrete data can be considered categorical and whether the traditional χ^2-test can be used. For example, suppose a child is asked the following question: "How much do you love your sister?" If the response is a fuzzy number (say, 70% of the time), it is certainly inappropriate to use the traditional χ^2-test for the analysis. We will present a χ^2-test for fuzzy data as follows:

3.3. Procedures for χ^2 -test with fuzzy categorical data

1. Sample: Let U be the universal set (a discussion domain), $L = \{L_1, L_2, \ldots, L_k\}$ a set of k-linguistic variables on U, and $\{A_1, A_2, \ldots, A_m\}$ and $\{B_1, B_2, \ldots, B_n\}$ two sets drawn from categorical populations with numbers on U. For each sample in $\{A_i, B_i\}$, assign a linguistic variable L_j and a normalised membership $m_{ij}(\sum_{j=1}^{k} m_{ij} = 1)$, and let $Fn_{ij} = \sum_{i \in A, B} Ln_{ij}i \in A, B; j = 1, 2, \ldots, k$ be the total memberships in the cell ij.

2. Hypothesis: Two populations have the same distribution ratio.
3. Statistics: $\chi^2 = \sum_{i \in A,B} \sum_{j=1}^{c} ([Fn_{ij}] - e^{ij})^2$ (In order to perform the Chi-square test for fuzzy data, we transfer the decimal fractions of Fn_{ij} in each cell of fuzzy category into the integer $[Fn_{ij}]$ by counting 5 and higher fractions as 1 and discard the rest.)
4. Decision rule: under significance level α, if $\chi^2 > \chi_\alpha^2(k-1)$, then we reject H_0.

4. Empirical Studies

4.1. *A general survey on the electricity market*

At present, Taiwanese investors are spread among the places in China such as Dongguan and Shenzhen the of Zhujiang Delta zone, while others prefer the Yangtze River Delta zone, such as Shanghai and Suzhou.

Most Taiwanese-invested industries have already formed an upstream and downstream supply chain in Yangtze River Delta area, and it comprised 55% of the (Integrated Circuit) CI manufacturer, 80% of IC packaging testing vendor and 50% of IC design house, this supply chain system already brought a tremendous development and growth for the IT industry in Yangtze River Delta area.[b] Aside from IC chips, all IT components can be built and assembled in Suzhou. Among six major IC manufacturers in China, five of them are situated in Yangtze River Delta area. From IC design, chip manufacturing, to packaging testing, it already forms a complete IC industry chain.

Electronic information industry was the first to invest in the Zhujiang Delta area. Its products in export accounted for the highest in the entire electronic information industry. Cities like Guangzhou, Dongguan, Shenzhen, and Huizhou already formed themselves into an "Electronic information Hall". These cities have already become a vital place for the Asia's electronic information industry, with a complete IT satellite manufacturing industry chain, and well integrated upstream, midstream and downstream supply chain that has gained recognition for its competitiveness in production. Taiwanese distributors will be responsible for R&D, getting purchase order, output production in mainland China and delivery in Hong Kong, this kind of supply chain system brings forth high-quality, low-cost products and gain

---

[b]"Top 100 Electric Enterprise Aggregated in the Three Major Economic Zones", Cheng peng, nanfangdushih newspaper, 2004-06-02, http://www.nanfangdaily.com.cn/southnews/tszk/nfdsb/smzk/200406020471.asp

an enormous number of orders and strategic partnerships from well-known global companies. For more than 10 years, Zhujiang's electronic information industry has the highest export value among cities in China. It has already become an important place of electronic information industry around the world.

We conducted a survey on Taiwanese businessmen who invested in China, 453 survey forms have been sent out, and we got 91 responses, a response rate of 20%.

4.2.   Satisfaction analysis

We make a comprehensive satisfactory statistic analysis based on the survey conducted on the Taiwanese IT vendors: Table 1 is "A comparison of traditional and fuzzy statistical analysis on industrial network benefits".

In the aspect of satisfaction for the benefits that the business industrial networks could: (a) reduce costs; (b) elevate its competitiveness; and (c) access more resources. The "whole mode" and "whole fuzzy mode" between those selections is 4, which is equal to "agree". The "whole degree of satisfaction" and "whole fuzzy degree of satisfaction" are around 3.5. Furthermore, the "whole degree of satisfaction" is higher than "whole fuzzy degree of satisfaction".

The results of the overall satisfaction conducted from the traditional type of survey is higher than fuzzy statistic method. On the other hand, the results of the survey show that the implementation of the business industrial network can deliver many benefits to the firm.

4.3.   The cross analysis

Followings are the results conducted from a cross-analysis of the network benefits.

There is no significant difference in marketing strength, production capability, raw material gains or logistic foundation wherever the industrial network is located. The locations built up by the business industrial network have different responses on the costs. The results of χ^2 which was derived from the traditional category analysis, is rejected. This indicates the degree of satisfaction on the cost reduction from different location established by the business industrial network is inconsistent. Nonetheless, based on the sample data we collected from the fuzzy category analysis, the result is acceptable. Such a result indicates both groups reached a certain degree of satisfaction.

Table 1. A comparison of traditional and fuzzy statistical analysis on industrial network benefits.

Network benefit	Traditional Category Analysis					Fuzzy Category Analysis				
	1*	2	3	4	5	1	2	3	4	5
Reduce costs Demand costs	4	7	16	42	22	4.5	10.1	22.7	33.4	20.1
Price costs	3	9	20	43	16	3.9	9.6	24.5	35.5	16.8
Supplies costs	4	9	23	38	17	4.4	11.2	26.1	31.9	17.5
Whole mode/ whole fuzzy mode	A little agrees with (123)					A little agrees with (100.7)				
Whole degree of satisfaction/whole fuzzy degree of satisfaction	3.68					$0.05/1+0.11/2+0.27/3+0.37/4+0.20/5$				
Elevate competitiveness Marketing strength	6	15	14	41	15	7.0	14.1	22.3	32.8	14.8
Research and development ability	9	16	22	33	10	8.8	18.2	25.2	25.8	11.7
Productivity	7	14	21	37	12	7.0	15.5	26.3	29.5	12.7
Whole mode/whole fuzzy mode	A little agrees with (111)					A little agrees with (88.1)				
Whole degree of satisfaction/whole fuzzy degree of satisfaction	3.34					$0.08/1+0.18/2+0.2/3+0.32/4+0.14/5$				

Table 1. (*Continued*)

Network benefit	Traditional Category Analysis					Fuzzy Category Analysis				
	1*	2	3	4	5	1	2	3	4	5
Access more resources	4	12	16	41	18	4.0	11.6	23.7	32.7	19
Raw material Logistic foundation	1	14	27	29	20	1.8	15.1	28.0	27.2	18.4
Whole mode/whole fuzzy mode	A little agrees with (70)					A little agrees with (59.9)				
Whole degree of satisfaction/whole fuzzy degree of satisfaction	3.60					$0.03/1+0.15/2+0.283+0.33/4+0.21/5$				

*1 = very disagree, 2 = disagree, 3 = medium, 4 = agree, 5 = very agree.

Table 2. Industrial network forms the place and the network benefits cross analysis

Satisfaction at $\alpha = 0.1$		Traditional category analysis						Fuzzy category analysis					
		1*	2	3	4	5	Chi-Square Test	1	2	3	4	5	Chi-Square Test
Demand costs	TW	3	6	10	29	14	$\chi^2 = 7.93$ $p = 0.094$ Reject	3.5	5.8	14.3	24.2	13.2	$\chi^2 = 3.76$ $p = 0.44$ Accept
Demand costs	TW	3	6	10	29	14	$\chi^2 = 7.93$ $p = 0.094$ Reject	3.5	5.8	14.3	24.2	13.2	$\chi^2 = 3.76$ $p = 0.44$ Accept
Marketing strength	CN	1	1	11	14	2	$\chi^2 = 3.16$ $p = 0.532$ Accept	0.4	3.8	10	11.3	3.6	$\chi^2 = 2.44$ $p = 0.66$ Accept
	TW	3	11	10	30	8		4.2	9.4	16.1	24.3	8.0	
R&D ability	CN	3	4	4	11	7	$\chi^2 = 10.05$ $p = 0.04$ Reject	2.8	4.7	6.20	8.5	6.8	$\chi^2 = 1.52$ $p = 0.82$ Accept
	TW	6	15	10	23	7		6.2	14.2	14.9	17.3	8.1	
Productivity	CN	3	1	12	10	3	$\chi^2 = 3.54$ $p = 0.47$ Accept	2.60	4.0	10.3	8.5	3.6	$\chi^2 = 0.48$ $p = 0.98$ Accept
	TW	4	11	12	25	10		4.2	10.8	17.0	20.7	9.3	
Raw material gains	CN	3	3	9	12	2	$\chi^2 = 4.6$ $p = 0.331$ Accept	2.8	4.7	9.30	8.80	3.4	$\chi^2 = 1.70$ $p = 0.79$ Accept
	TW	3	11	9	28	11		3.2	9.6	15.9	21.4	11.9	
Logistic foundation	CN	1	1	7	13	7	$\chi^2 = 4.17$ $p = **$	0.80	2.0	7.80	11.3	7.10	$\chi^2 = 2.4$ $p = **$
	TW	1	11	16	19	15		1.40	12.0	17.5	17.6	13.5	
	CN	0	3	11	10	3		0.40	3.10	10.5	9.60	4.90	

*1=very disagree, 2=disagree, 3=medium, 4=agree, 5=very agree.

**2 cells with expected counts less than 1. 3 cells with expected counts less than 5. Chi-Square approximation probably invalid.

Similarly, the result shown from Table 2 on the R&D ability, i.e., there is a significant difference in the R&D ability whether the industrial network is formed in Taiwan or China from traditional category analysis, is rejected. In other words, the degree of satisfaction is inconsistent between two parties. On the contrary, there is no significant difference when using fuzzy category analysis. It indicates that both parties show the similar degree of satisfaction on this point.

In conclusion, that discrepancy that arises between both analyses may be due to the uncertainty in human thoughts in fuzzy category analysis, such as not having enough time or "irresponsible" answering, and variation may arise.

5. Conclusion

In a survey of members of industrial network, we find the members are satisfied with the benefits from the industrial network in both whole satisfaction and fuzzy whole satisfaction.

Analysis that the questionnaire was designed for the fuzzy characteristic of numerical data by using fuzzy statistical methods will be more convincing than that by traditional statistical methods. This is because the traditional method can be overridden to get the higher score, while the fuzzy method will get the lower score. The fuzzy statistical method is more objective than the traditional one. Furthermore, using the fuzzy statistical method can lead to real or specific situations. For example, certain locations of industrial networks can decrease transaction costs and increase industrial competitiveness and best utilisation of industrial resources. In addition, for the location of the industrial network, the traditional and the fuzzy statistical methods will have different results.

This survey research is based upon some underlying assumptions or factors and therefore further studies can be made:

(1) Do advanced research in fuzzy expected values, fuzzy medians, and fuzzy variance.
(2) Invite psychologists to be team members to evaluate the consistency between thoughts and behaviors.
(3) Develop programs of fuzzy software which can help increase the efficiency of data-collecting and computing, so as to be more effective in automating fuzzy statistical methods and to overcome the greater difficulties inherent in fuzzy statistical methods.

(4) For consideration of industrial network benefit, there will be a large variance for different industries, areas, enterprise sizes, and time periods. This study only focuses on the electronic information industry. As for comparison between different industries in sizes and areas, further study is needed.

References

Guariso, G, A Rizzoli and H Werthner (1992). Identif ication of model structure via qualitive simulation. *IEEE Trans. on Systems, Man, and Cybernetics*, 22(5), 1075–1086.

Jarillo, JC (1998). On strategic networks. *Strategic Management Journal*, 9, 31–41.

Ruspini, E (1991). Approximate reasoning: Past, present, future. *Information Science*, 57, 297–317.

Tseng, T and C Klein (1992). A new algorithm for fuzzy multicriteria decision making. *International Journal of Approximate Reasoning*, 6, 45–66.

Wu, B and N Tseng (2002). A new approach to fuzzy regression models with application to business cycle analysis. *Fuzzy Sets and System*, 130, 33–42.

Wu, B and YY Hsu (2004). A new approach of bivariate fuzzy time series: With applications to the stock index forecasting. *International Journal of Uncertainty, Fuzziness and Knowledge-based systems*, 11(6), 671–690.

Zadeh, LA (1965). "Fuzzy Sets", *Information and Control*, 8, 1965, 338–353.

5

AN EXAMINATION OF DETERMINANTS OF LIKELIHOOD OF CONSIDERATION OF COUNTERFEIT LUXURY BRANDED PRODUCTS

Xuemei Bian

University of Hull, UK

This study examines the determinants of likelihood of consideration of counterfeit branded luxury handbags in the context of nondeceptive counterfeiting. The effects of consumer-perceived brand personality, benefits, product attributes, perceived risks, and consumer demographic variables are anticipated and explored. Focus groups are used to generate criteria which consumers used to evaluate studied brands, and an interview survey is used to collect data for the main study. SPSS and R software are used to analyze data. Generalised linear model analyses reveal that the brand personality is the dominant factor in determining the likelihood of the consideration of the counterfeit branded luxury products. In general, the perceived risks and the demographic variables do not appear to be significantly influential on the formation of the consideration set in the context of nondeceptive counterfeiting. In addition, factor analysis results provide empirical evidence on Plummer's (2000, 1985). Brand image components notion and further suggest that the perceived risks shall not be regarded as part of the benefit/consequence component of brand image concept.

Keywords: Counterfeit; brand personality; perceived risk; consideration set.

1. Background

Branding activities are no longer supportive functions but rather the essence of business (Salzer-Mörling, 2004). The objective of investing in brand development is to create a complex entity that lives in the consumer's mind (de Chernatony, 1993), around which products come to be recognised and

77

valued by customers, and customer loyalty is built (Erdem and Swait, 1998; Rao *et al.*, 1999). Successful branded goods usually demand a higher price in the marketplace; thus, brand is regarded as a critical intangible asset of a company (de Chernatony, 1993). In fact, global or national brands are the main creators of wealth (Hopkins *et al.*, 2003; Perrier, 1997). Unfortunately, the success of a branded product can breed counterfeiting to the extent that competitive offerings may be designed to appear indistinguishable from the original they mimic (Cordell *et al.*, 1996).

Counterfeiting is defined in many different ways. The most commonly accepted definition of counterfeits are those bearing a trademark that is identical to, or indistinguishable from, a trademark registered to another party, thus infringing on the rights of the holder of the trademark (e.g., Bian and Veloutsou, 2007, 2004; Chaudhry and Walsh, 1996; Kapferer, 1995; Grossman and Shapiro, 1988a, b). Although counterfeiting is not new, it had never been such a serious concern to national governments, supranational organisations, and legitimate manufacturers until the 1970s. Harvey and Ronkainen (1985) state that counterfeiting has been a problem for a long time, yet, it was only in the 1970s that it mushroomed. Globally, the sales of counterfeit products are estimated to be about $300 billion (Gentry *et al.*, 2001; Chaudhry and Walsh, 1996). The International Chamber of Commerce states that counterfeits account for 8% of world trade (Freedman, 1999). No product categories are left unscathed; counterfeiting has become a significant economic phenomenon in last 2 decades (Shultz II and Saporito, 1996). Counterfeiting is growing rapidly and that the growth will continue (Bian, 2006).

In line with its fast growth, the counterfeiting phenomenon has attracted more and more research interest recently (see Bian, 2006, for details). It is argued that consumer demand for counterfeit brands is one of the leading causes of the existence and upsurge in the growth of the counterfeiting phenomenon, given that demand is always the key driver of a market (e.g., Gentry *et al.*, 2001; Grossman and Shapiro, 1988a). This argument has been appreciated by several researchers, who suggested that further investigation of consumer behaviour and counterfeits was needed (e.g., Bian, 2006; Penz and Stöttinger, 2003; Wee *et al.*, 1995; Bloch *et al.*, 1993).

Past research in the study of consumers and counterfeits mainly focuses on profiling counterfeit-prone consumers (e.g., Bloch *et al.*, 1993; Tom *et al.*, 1998; Phau *et al.*, 2001; Wee *et al.*, 1995; Ang *et al.*, 2001); examining consumers perceptions and attitudes towards counterfeits (e.g., Bamossy and Scammon, 1985; Bloch *et al.*, 1993; Nia and Zaichkowsky, 2000; Penz and

Stöttinger, 2003; Bian and Veloutsou, 2006); investigating whether or not consumers purchase counterfeits (e.g., Hoe *et al.*, 2003; Bloch *et al.*, 1993; Wee *et al.*, 1995; Tom *et al.*, 1998; Phau *et al.*, 2001; Cordell and Wongtada, 1991; Gentry *et al.*, 2001; Harvey and Walls, 2003), exploring the factors that determine consumer purchase behaviour of counterfeits (e.g., Dodge *et al.*, 1996; Bloch *et al.*, 1993; Wee *et al.*, 1995; Cordell *et al.*, 1996; Albers-Miller, 1999; Phau *et al.*, 2001; Chakraborty *et al.*, 1996; Chabraborty *et al.*, 1997; Penz and Stöttinger, 2005).

A counterfeit must copy a trademarked brand that is appealing to consumers (Cordell *et al.*, 1996). Prior researchers recommend that if branded products did not attract consumers, counterfeiting would not be an issue (e.g., Cordell *et al.*, 1996; Bloch *et al.*, 1993). Successful branded products have the highest level of attractiveness to counterfeiters (Harvey and Ronkainen, 1985), with luxury brands appearing to be more likely to be counterfeited than other generic brands (Green and Smith, 2002). Despite the close connection between a brand and a counterfeit product, little attention has been placed on examination of consumer behaviour and counterfeits from a brand perspective.

The current study investigates, in the context of nondeceptive counterfeiting (NDC), effects of consumer-perceived brand image (brand personalities, product attributes, benefits/consequences) and perceived risks of counterfeit luxury branded products (CLBP) on likelihood of consideration of these products. Here, NDC refers to the practice of consumers knowingly purchasing counterfeits (Grossman and Shapiro, 1988a). The choice of the NDC context is considered important, because under these circumstances it is possible to be able to measure consumers' perceptions of counterfeit branded products more precisely.

2. Theoretical Development and Hypotheses

2.1. *Brand image*

Brand image is "how a brand is perceived by consumers" (Aaker, 1996, p. 71). Brand image is important because it contributes to the consumer's decision about whether or not the brand is the one for him/her (Dolich, 1969) and it influences consumers' subsequent buying behaviour (Johnson and Puto, 1987; Fishbein, 1967). Plummer (2000, 1985) suggests product attributes, the benefits/consequences of using a brand, and brand personality are the three key components of brand image. Factor analysis results of the current research provide empirical support to Plummer's brand image component notion (see the Research Results section). As such, the following provides conceptualisation of these constructs as well as related hypotheses.

2.2. Brand personality

The brand personality factor enables a consumer to express his/her own self (Hem and Iversen, 2002; Aaker, 1999) or specific dimensions of the self (Kleine et al., 1993); it serves as a symbolic or self-expressive function, and it helps consumers differ from or integrate themselves with others (Keller, 1993). It also projects the brands' values and creates an image of the brand's typical user (de Chernatony and McDonald, 1998; Johar and Sirgy, 1991), which might be the ideal image of the consumer. This brand information may actually encourage the use of a given brand as a self-expressive device by consumers who hold a similar position and want to present a similar image or ideal self (Malhotra, 1988).

Past research suggests that favourable brand personality is a central driver of consumer preference and usage (Freling and Forbes, 2005; Biel, 1993; Batra et al., 1993; Sirgy, 1982), as consumers are more likely to associate them with a desired group, or self-image (Aaker, 1997; Lefkoff-Hagius and Mason, 1993). If previous research findings still hold true in the context of NDC, one should expect that when CLBPs are perceived to project a positive and favourable brand personality, they are more likely to be included in the consideration set. Thus, the following hypothesis is proposed.

H1: The level of consumers' favourableness to the brand personality of CLBPs has a positive relationship to the likelihood of the consideration of the CLBPs.

2.3. Product attributes

Product attributes can be categorised in a variety of ways (Myers and Shocker, 1981). Keller's (1993) broad view suggests that product attributes are those descriptive features that characterise a product. Stokmans's (1991) narrow view indicates that a product can be viewed as a bundle of intrinsic and extrinsic attributes, or as a bundle of perceived attributes. The intrinsic attributes of the product are information cues directly linked to the product, and those extrinsic attributes are information cues which are indirectly connected to the product (Stokmans, 1991). This research takes Stokmans's viewpoint of the product attributes, as it is consistent with a number of previous studies (e.g., Romaniuk, 2003; Holden, 1993).

The consumer uses perceived attributes in the decision-making process (Puth *et al.*, 1999). Positive relationships between linkages of the brand and the perceived product attributes, and brand choice/preference has been found by multiple researchers since 1960s (e.g., Nedungadi, 1990; Cohen, 1966; Axelrod, 1968), which indicate that the more positive the consumers' perceptions of the product attributes of a specific brand, the more chance there is of the branded product being considered. As such, this research proposes the following.

H2: The consumers' perceptions of product attributes of CLBPs have a positive influence on the likelihood of the consideration of the CLBPs.

2.4. Perceived benefits

Benefits are what consumers seek when purchasing a product/brand (Kotler, 1999; Puth *et al.*, 1999). These benefits lead to certain end states or values that consumers wish to achieve (Kotler, 1999; Belch and Belch, 1995; Peter and Olson, 1994; Mowen, 1993; Aaker *et al.*, 1992). Perceived benefit is what consumers think the product can do for them (Keller, 1993); it is associated with perception of product attributes and brand personality. In relation to CLBPs, the perceived benefits are what consumers believe the CLBPs can bring them.

Numerous previous studies have demonstrated a positive relationship between perceived benefit and consumer decision-making (e.g., Cho *et al.*, 2002; Bove and Johnson, 2000; Mai and Ness, 1997; Dodge *et al.*, 1996). Prior research reveals that consumers who willfully buy CLBPs believe they are getting the prestige (e.g., Ang *et al.*, 2001; Tom *et al.*, 1998; Bloch *et al.*, 1993) and quality (Grossman and Shapiro, 1988a) of the original branded product (BP) for a fraction of its price (Tom *et al.*, 1998). Accordingly, the proposed hypothesis is as follows:

H3: The consumers' perceptions of the benefits of CLBPs have a positive influence on the likelihood of the consideration of the CLBPs.

2.5. Perceived risks

Perceived risk has been regarded as one of the major explanatory variables in consumer behaviour (Mitchell, 1999; Mitchell and Boustani, 1993; Gabbott,

1991; Brooker, 1984). It has for a long time been acknowledged in the marketing literature as an important issue during buying decisions, suggesting that consumers seek to reduce uncertainty and unfavourable consequences of purchase decisions (Mitchell, 1999; Cox, 1967; Bauer, 1960).

Perceived risk comprises multidimensional constructs (Mandel, 2003; Campbell and Goodstein, 2001; Mitchell and Boustani, 1993; Jacoby and Kaplan, 1972; Roselius, 1971; Cox, 1967; Cunningham, 1967). The focus group data revealed that in the context of NDC, consumers are mainly concerned about social risk, financial risk and performance risk. The performance risk is embedded in the "long-lasting" factor. As a result, of interest to this study, only the social risk, and financial risk are discussed in detail.

Consumers may face more financial risk in buying CLBPs than BPs, due to the high uncertainty of their performance and unlikelihood of consumer redress (Cordell *et al.*, 1996; Bamossy and Scammon, 1985). Consumers are concerned about being found out by their peers or people whom they esteem that they are buying and using counterfeit branded products (Wee *et al.*, 1995). In addition, the focus group data revealed that consumers are also worried they might be singled out by peers for purchasing CLBPs. Thus, it is expected that greater perceived risk should reduce consumers' likelihood of consideration of CLBPs. The following hypothesis is formulated.

H4: The level of consumer perceived risk of CLBPs has a negative relationship to the likelihood of the consideration of the CLBPs.

3.   Research Methodology

3.1.   *Brands examined*

A review of previous work on study of consumer demand side of the counterfeiting phenomenon show that a number of researchers have investigated product categories in their studies (e.g., Nia and Zaichkowsky, 2000; Phau *et al.*, 2001; Harvey and Walls, 2003; Bian and Veloutsou, 2004). Few studies examine specific brands, with the exception of that of Cordell and Wongtada (1991), which examines the impact of specified brands on consumers' judgment of whether or not a product is counterfeit. Given that consumer behaviour is pretty much brand- and product-specified, it is rational to question the applicability of previous research findings based on investigation of product categories on specific brands. Hence, for this research, specific brands are examined because using specific brands can help subjects to achieve a better understanding of the studied objects, and can also fill the identified literature gap, i.e., lack of research in the study of counterfeiting phenomenon related to the investigation of specific brands.

Two luxury handbag brands (Louis Vuitton and Burberry) are tested in this study. These brands are chosen because they are well-known and long-established brands, and thus familiar to the targeted respondents; these brands are on the list of the most counterfeited brands (Poulter, 2006); the counterfeit versions of these brands are available and appear to be more acceptable to consumers than other counterfeits (Anti-Counterfeiting Group Survey Report, 2004). It is considered to be essential to ensure that the studied brands are accessible and acceptable to the target population to some extent, and have a high degree of consumer awareness. If any of the conditions do not hold, then there is no chance that consumers will knowingly purchase them. Consequently, the research aim will appear pointless both theoretically and practically.

The development of the research instrument proceeded in three phases before it is used to collect data. The first phase involving two focus group discussions aims to generate criteria used by consumers to evaluate studied CLBPs. Content analysis is used to extract the most relevant and important criteria used by participants in evaluating the studied CLBPs in the consideration process. In total, 27 items are extracted for Burberry and 26 for Louis Vuitton (see Appendix for details). The extracted criteria form the measure of consumer perceptions towards the selected CLBPs. Troye's (1983) 5-item scale is adopted to measure the regressed variable, consideration set, with necessary adaptation.

The second and third phases consist of two questionnaire pretests. Three academic researchers not involved directly in the design of the questionnaire but who are familiar with questionnaire design principles and have knowledge of the subjects are interviewed by the researcher aiming to detect technical errors. Then, the questionnaire is tested on 40 consumers to identify potential problems related to mode of administration, individual questions, and question sequences. Identified deficiencies are dealt with carefully, which results in a robust and user-friendly research instrument.

The self-administered questionnaire mainly comprises Likert 5-point scales with end-anchors (1 = strongly disagree, 5 = strongly agree). The definition of counterfeiting adopted for this study is displayed on the cover page of the questionnaire in an attempt to ensure that the participants have a universal understanding of this terminology. The information that "one-third of British people knowingly purchase counterfeit branded products" (Anti-Counterfeiting Group Survey Report, 2004) is also provided, aiming to encourage participants to provide truthful information, as it is believed that this technique can make it easier for the respondent to admit to potentially embarrassing behaviour (Churchill, 1999).

3.2. *Sample*

A stimulus-approach is adopted in this research. Specifically, counterfeit Burberry and Louis Vuitton handbags are presented to respondents. An interview survey is used to collect data. The data are collected from four randomly selected supermarkets in December 2006 in Glasgow. Every *n*th shopper is invited to participate in this research at the exit of the supermarkets rather than in the supermarkets to avoid length-biased sampling (Nowell and Stanley, 1991). The gaze and touch method recommended by Hornik and Ellis (1988), the appealing verbal method suggested by Hornik (1982), together with the traditional incentive method (a box of chocolates worth about £2.50) are adopted to reduce nonresponse rate.

In total, 277 completed questionnaires were collected. Of the 277 respondents, 96 are men and 181 are women. 64 are younger than 20, 64 are between 21 and 30, 56 are between 31 and 40, 57 are between 41 and 50, and 36 are over 50 years old. 95 have high school or lower educational background, 70 with Higher National Diploma/Higher National Certificate, 76 with Bachelor of Arts/Masters of Arts, 35 with Masters degree, 56 with a household income lower than £10,000 per year, 79 between £10,000 and £24,999, 58 between £25,000 and £39,999, and 67 with household income higher than £40,000.

4. Research Results

Data are analysed using the SPSS program and R commander. The dimensionality of consumers' perceptions of each brand is assessed using Principal Component Analysis (PCA) with varimax rotation. The PCA is utilised because the researcher is only interested in data reduction at this stage, and the PCA is often preferred as a method for data reduction over Principal Factor Analysis (PFA) (Preacher and MacCallum, 2003). The PFA and Cronbach Alpha (Pearson Correlation Analysis, if applicable) are used to validate adopted scales. The PFA is appropriate as it is often preferred when the goal of the analysis is to detect structure (Caruso and Cliff, 1998). A generalised linear model (GLM) analysis is conducted to test the hypothesis of this study.

4.1. PCA results

In both cases, KMO values are greater than 0.80, which are classified as "great" (Kaier, 1974). All factors with an eigenvalue greater than 1.0 and factor loadings of at least 0.4 are reported. Five factors were extracted for both Burberry and Louis Vuitton data, which account for 59.43% of the overall variance (Table 1) for Burberry, and 64.14% for Louis Vuitton (Table 2). The results indicate a clear three-component structure of the brand image construct. Specifically, the five factors can be categorised into three groups in both cases. These categories are brand personality, product attribute (general product attribute, and price and material), and benefit/consequence (image benefit, and long-lasting benefit) with the first two factors explaining 48% of the variance for Burberry; brand personality, product attribute (general product attribute and price), and benefit/consequence (image benefit and long-last benefit), with the first two factors accounting for 53% of the variance explained by all extracted factors for Louis Vuitton.

Most of the pattern loadings in both solutions are quite high in the contribution of the original variables to the formation of new factors, ranging from 0.637 to 0.869 (with the exception of two items) in the case of Burberry, while in the case of Louis Vuitton, these loadings range from 0.604 to 0.880 (with the exception of two cases). Item 7 (high quality) and 13 (exclusivity) are dropped off in both cases, due to them not appearing to fit in with any extracted factors. It is believed that the item "high quality" is too general in comparison with other tested items, whereas "exclusivity" is just something consumers cannot associate with the examined CLBPs.

Items related to social risk and financial risk do not fit in with any extracted factors in either case. In fact, they interfere with extraction of factors. Social and financial risks might correlate to other brand image dimensions (e.g., image and long-last benefits), but theoretically they are well-defined constructs and differ from items related to the brand image construct. Thus, the exclusion of these items from the PCA makes theoretical sense. The PCA results provide empirical support to Plummer's (2000, 1985) brand image three-component notion and suggest the perceived risk shall not be regarded as a sub-dimension of benefit/consequence.

Table 1.   Extracted Burberry image factors.

No.	Items	Counterfeit Burberry				
		1	2	3	4	5
1	I can get the size I want.		0.708			
2	It is expensive.				0.869	
3	The materials are good.				0.695	
4	They have the style I like.		0.810			
5	They have the color I like.		0.847			
6	The product is practical.		0.750			
7	In buying this version, you get a high standard of quality.	—	—	—	—	—
8	The product is a statement of your self-image.			0.740		
9	This product can bring you fun.			0.637		
10	The quality of the product merits the price.			0.727		
11	In buying this product, you get value for money for the status it brings you.			0.659		
12	You can throw it away after a while.					0.738
13	This product brings you exclusivity.	—	—	—	—	—
14	This product can make you attract other people's attention.			0.717		
15	This product might not last long.					0.799
18	Down to earth	0.474				
19	Original	0.774				
20	Unique	0.779				
21	Contemporary	0.699				
22	Reliable	0.711				
23	Corporate	0.743				
24	Successful	0.714				
25	Feminine	0.695				
26	Outdoorsy	0.569				
KMO				0.85		
Cumulated variance explained %				59.43		
Eigenvalue		6.00	2.72	1.82	1.45	1.08
% of variance		27.27	12.35	8.29	6.60	4.92
Cronbach α		0.87	0.83	0.77	0.51[a]	0.38[a]
% of nonredundant residuals with absolute values greater than 0.05				30		

[a]Pearson correlation is reported, and significant at 0.01 (2-tails).

Table 2. Extracted LV brand image factors.

No.	Items	Counterfeit LV				
		1	2	3	4	5
1	I can get the size I want.			0.640		
2	It is expensive.					0.868
3	The materials are good.			0.433		0.599
4	They have the style I like.			0.876		
5	I can get the color I want.			0.880		
6	The product is practical.			0.785		
7	In buying this version, you get a high standard of quality.	—	—	—	—	—
8	The product is a statement of your self-image.	0.654				
9	This product can bring you fun.	0.644				
10	The quality of the product merits the price.	0.604				
11	In buying this product, you get value for money for the status it brings you.	0.711				
12	You can throw it away after a while.				0.808	
13	This product brings you exclusivity.	—	—	—	—	—
14	This product can make you attract other people's attention.	0.787				
15	This product can bring you prestige.	0.654				
16	This product might not last long.				0.782	
17	This product gives people impression that what you wear is fashionable.	0.725				
18	Trendy		0.688			
19	Contemporary		0.689			
20	Successful		0.753			
21	Upper class		0.745			
22	Feminine		0.772			
23	Smooth		0.795			
KMO				0.87		
Cumulated variance explained %				64.14		
Eigenvalue		6.79	2.29	2.08	1.28	1.04
% of variance		32.31	10.91	9.88	6.10	4.94
Cronbach α		0.85	0.87	0.86	0.39[a]	—
% of nonredundant residuals with absolute values greater than 0.05				26		

[a]Pearson correlation is reported, and significant at 0.01 (2-tails).

4.2.   Reliability and validity results

The Cronbach Alpha values for all extracted factors of both the Burberry and Louis Vuitton brands are all greater than 0.70, which is the acceptable level suggested by Hinkin (1995). Whenever the Pearson Correlation is applicable, the results show that the correlations are significant at the 0.01 level (two-tailed) (Tables 1 and 2).

A one-factor solution is appropriate based on a minimum eigenvalue of 1 for the consideration set construct of both brands, with factor loading ranges between 0.60 and 0.90 for Burberry, and 0.72 to 0.90 for Louis Vuitton (Table 3). The variances explained by the one-factor are 72.1% (Burberry) and 75% (Louis Vuitton). The KMO values are categorised as great (0.85 and 0.88). Thus, scale of the consideration set is mono-dimensional. Accordingly, a conclusion can be drawn that the measurements this research adopted are reliable and valid.

4.3.   GLM results

Considering the fact that the response variables and the residuals are positively skewed, it is expected that transforming the response variable data down the ladder of powers will have a positive influence on the model (Fox, 2002). Therefore, the response variables are transformed first. Regressions are run based on the transformed response variable data. Nevertheless, the transformation of the response variables data does not appear to have great

Table 3.   Factor solution of consideration set.

Consideration set (handbags)	Factor loading		% of variance explained		KMO	
	CB	CLV	CB	CLV	CB	CLV
I would consider buying one these handbags.	0.90	0.86	72.1	75.0	0.85	0.88
I would recommend these handbags.	0.85	0.85				
These handbags are attractive to me.	0.90	0.90				
These handbags are acceptable of purchase.	0.77	0.81				
These handbags are acceptable within the price range I am willing to pay.	0.60	0.72				

Extraction Method: Principal Axis Factoring. A one factor extracted. CB = Counterfeit Burberry; CLV = Counterfeit Louis Vuitton.

positive influence on the models in the case of either Burberry or Louis Vuitton. Therefore, the explanatory variables data are transformed as well after the transformation of the response variables data. If still no clear improvement was achieved, further test takes place on transforming the explanatory variables data solely. Box-Cox and Box-Tidwell transformation techniques were utilised to implement data transformation of the response variables data and the explanatory variables data. Regressions are rerun based on the transformed data. Investigations are carried out on the impact of the various transformations on the models. The most improved models are presented together with their corresponding initial models generated before any transformation is conducted (Tables 4 and 5).

Data transformation does not appear to have remarkable impact on the models. The improvement of F-statistics is 6.59 for Burberry and 0.43 for Louis Vuitton, with adjusted R^2 improved by 0.04 for Burberry (Table 4) and 0.001 for Louis Vuitton (Table 5). Considering data transformations do not seem to improve the models much, and interpreting the transformed model is practically difficult, it is sensible to retain and interpret the GLM models (initial models) that are not involved in any transformation.

4.4. Likelihood of consideration results for counterfeit Burberry

Five exploratory variables are statistically significant at better than $a = 0.01$, and account for an adjusted R^2 of 0.154 of the likelihood of consideration of counterfeit Burberry (Table 4). The model suggests that such likelihood of consideration is a function of perceived brand personality ($\beta = 0.28$, $p < 0.00$), image benefit ($\beta = 0.15$, $p < 0.00$), practical attributes ($\beta = 0.14$, $p < 0.00$), long-lasting benefit ($\beta = -0.11$, $p < 0.01$), and social risk ($\beta = -0.11$, $p < 0.00$).

The brand personality comes before any other explanatory variable in determining the likelihood of the consideration of the counterfeit Burberry. This implies that the perceived brand personality plays a very important role in the model. The perceived image benefit is the second most influential variable followed by the perceived practical attributes. The positive coefficient values indicate a positive relationship to the consideration of the counterfeit Burberry.

The long-lasting benefit exerts a negative influence on the consideration of the counterfeit Burberry. The long-lasting benefit factor consists of product life and disposability. The negative value of the coefficient implies that consumers who are more likely to consider purchasing counterfeit Burberry

Table 4. Comparison of the initial generalised linear model and the generalised linear model after transformation (Counterfeit Burberry likelihood of consideration).

Initial generalised linear model *before* any transformation

Variables entered	T to enter	Significance	Multiple R^2	Adjusted R^2	Overall F^*
Personality	5.34	0.000	0.170	0.154	11.06
Product attributes	2.74	0.001			
Image benefit	2.78	0.001			
Long-lasting benefit	−1.98	0.01			
Social risk	−2.11	0.01			

Regression equation *before* any transformation

	B	SE B	T	Significant
Personality	0.28	0.05	5.34	0.000
Product attributes	0.14	0.05	2.74	0.001
Image benefit	0.15	0.05	2.78	0.001
Long-lasting benefit	−0.11	0.05	−1.98	0.01
Social risk	−0.09	0.04	−2.11	0.01
Constant	2.05	0.13	15.36	0.000

Generalised linear model *after* transformation of *response variable and explanatory variables*

	Power	T to enter	Significance	Multiple R^2	Adjusted R^2	Overall F^*
Personality	0.14	−5.43	0.000	0.206	0.194	17.65
Product attributes	0.89	−3.34	0.000			
Image benefit	−0.96	3.60	0.000			
Long-lasting benefit	7.22	3.13	0.001			
Consideration[1]	−0.8	—	—			

Regression equation *after* transformation of *response variable and explanatory variables*

	Power	B	SE B	T	Significant
Personality	0.14	−7.76e − 01	1.43e − 01	−5.43	0.000
Product attributes	0.89	−5.69e − 02	1.70e − 02	−3.34	0.000
Image benefit	−0.96	2.72e − 01	7.56e − 02	3.60	0.000
Long-lasting benefit	7.22	1.02e − 06	3.24e − 07	3.13	0.001
Constant	—	1.59e + 00	—	9.48	0.000

— NA.
[1]Response variable.
[2]Interaction of product knowledge and product involvement.
*The overall Fs are significant at 0.000 level.

are less likely to expect that the counterfeit version will last long. In other words, counterfeit-prone consumers might be attracted by the disposable nature of the CLBPs.

The social risk also has a significant explanatory power on the likelihood of the consideration of the counterfeit Burberry. The negative beta value suggests that the higher the level of social risk the subjects perceive in relation

Table 5. Comparison of the initial generalised linear model and the generalised linear model after transformation (Counterfeit Louis Vuitton likelihood of consideration).

Initial generalised linear model *before* any transformation

Variables entered	T to enter	Significance	Multiple R^2	Adjusted R^2	Overall F^*
Image benefit	5.20	0.000	0.32	0.30	25.18
Personality	6.22	0.000			
Product attributes	5.80	0.000			
Long-lasting benefit	−4.22	0.000			
Gender (male dummy coded)	−2.22	0.05			

Regression equation *before* any transformation

	B	SE B	T	Significant
Image benefit	0.27	0.05	5.20	0.000
Personality	0.33	0.05	6.22	0.000
Product attributes	0.031	0.05	5.80	0.000
Long-lasting benefit	−0.22	0.05	−4.22	0.000
Gender (male dummy coded)	0.25	0.11	−2.22	0.05
Constant	2.03	0.07	31.21	0.000

Generalised Linear Model *after* transformation of *explanatory variables*

	Power	T to enter	Significance	Multiple R^2	Adjusted R^2	Overall F^*
Image benefit	1.47	5.07	0.000	0.321	0.301	25.61
Personality	0.89	6.34	0.000			
Product attributes	0.57	5.90	0.000			
Long-lasting benefit	2.20	−4.33	0.000			
Gender (male dummy coded)	—	−2.28	0.05			

Regression equation *after* transformation of *explanatory variables*

	Power	B	SE B	T	Significant
Image benefit	1.47	0.10	0.19	5.07	0.000
Personality	0.89	0.44	0.69	6.34	0.000
Product attributes	0.57	0.99	0.17	5.90	0.000
Long-lasting benefit	2.20	−0.02	0.005	−4.33	0.000
Gender (male dummy coded)	—	−0.25	0.11	−2.28	0.05
Constant	—	−1.88	0.48	−3.94	0.000

— NA.
*The overall *F*s are significant at 0.000 level.

to the counterfeit Burberry, the less likely it is that they will consider buying it. This is in line with the risk-averse theory.

4.5. *Likelihood of consideration results for counterfeit Louis Vuitton*

Five variables account for an adjusted R^2 of 0.30 in explaining the subjects' likelihood of consideration of this version of the counterfeit Louis Vuitton handbag (Table 5). The model suggests that such likelihood of consideration is a function of brand personality (β = 0.33, p < 0.00), image benefit (β = 0.27, p < 0.00), product attributes (β = 0.031, p < 0.00), long-lasting benefit (β = −0.22, p < 0.00), and gender (β = −0.25, p < 0.05).

Identical to the Burberry model, the brand personality is found to have the most impact on the subjects' likelihood of consideration of the counterfeit Louis Vuitton, with the perceived image benefit as the second explanatory power. The perceived product attributes, although still significantly influential, nevertheless, have an explanatory power which is considered to be very limited, judging by the small beta value.

The perceived long-lasting benefit appears to be the third most powerful explanatory variable to the model. The coefficient value is also negative, which suggests a negative relation to the response variable. The reasoning provided in the Burberry section should be applicable. Therefore, no more explanation is offered here. Gender is only significant at 0.05 level. The negative value implies that males are less likely to consider purchasing counterfeit Louis Vuitton in comparison to females, as female is coded as the reference variable.

5.   Discussion and Conclusion

5.1.   *Summary of findings*

From the GLM results, it can be seen that the perceived brand personality of the CLBPs performs best among the tested variables in explaining consumers' likelihood of consideration of these products (Hypothesis 1 is fully supported). This clearly implies that a critical role is played by the perceived brand personality in the consideration process of consumer behaviour in relation to CLBPs. The perceived image benefit features prominently in the set of the determinants of the consideration of CLBPs (Hypothesis 2 is supported). Nevertheless, in both models this sub-construct of the perceived image benefit comes after the perceived brand personality in terms of explanatory power (judged on beta values). In contrast to expectation, the perceived long-lasting benefit shows significant but negative effect on the likelihood of consideration of the CLBPs in both models, which implies that counterfeit-prone consumers are attracted by the disposable nature of the CLBPs (Hypothesis 2 is partially rejected). This is in line with Gentry *et al.* (2006) who suggest that counterfeits are easily replaced and relatively cheap for consumers to stay current are among the reasons consumers willingly purchase counterfeit fashionable products.

The general product attributes also have significant effect on the likelihood of consideration of the CLBPs. Nevertheless, the magnitude of its influence is limited in comparison with the perceived brand personality and the image benefit (Hypothesis 3 is supported). Despite numerous researches recommending that low price is one of the key determinants for purchase of counterfeits (e.g., Gentry *et al.*, 2006; Phau *et al.*, 2001.), the current research reveals that there is no relationship between perceived price and the likelihood of consideration of the CLBPs (Hypothesis 3 is partially rejected). The unexpected result can be explained by the commonly perceived very low price (with a mean of 1.97 for Burberry and 1.92 for Louis Vuitton) of the examined versions of the CLBPs. In the present study, both perceived benefits and perceived product attributes are bio-dimensional constructs; both have a nonuniform effect on the likelihood of consideration of the CLBPs, depending on the type of the perceived benefit and the type of the perceived product attribute.

Gentry *et al.* (2006) found that consumers purchase counterfeits as they really want the "brand". Nevertheless, Gentry *et al.* (2006) did not provide further information with regard to what "brand" represents in their research. The current research goes beyond previous studies. This research highlights that predominately counterfeit-prone consumers are appealed to primarily by the perceived brand personality of the CLBPs, followed by the perceived image benefit. In addition, the counterfeit-prone consumers are also after the perceived general product attributes (size, style, color, and practicality) of the CLBPs which are directly copied from the BPs.

In general, the financial risk and the social risk do not have significant effects on the consumers' likelihood of consideration of the CLBPs, with the exception of social risk concerning counterfeit Burberry handbags. One should be aware that here the social risk refers to "fear of being singled out by society". This research believes that the significantly negative relationship is caused by the contaminated Burberry image rather than the nature of the counterfeit version. Therefore, the research results disconfirm Hypothesis 4.

The demographics do not show a significant effect on the consideration of counterfeits with the exception of gender for Louis Vuitton data. The results related to age support Bloch *et al.* (1993) and Wee *et al.*'s (1995) research findings, but are contradictory to those of Tom *et al.* (1998), who claim a negative relationship between age and consumer purchase behaviour of counterfeits. The education-related results are in line with those of Phau *et al.* (2001) and Bian and Veloutsou (2007), but different to those of Wee *et al.* (1995). Income is not significantly influential on the likelihood of consideration of the CLBPs. This finding differs from that of Tom *et al.* (1998) who claim that consumer accomplices of counterfeits are more likely to have lower incomes; nevertheless, it is in the same vein of that of Blotch *et al.* (1993) who report that income is not effective in distinguishing between counterfeit accomplices and consumers who would choose BPs.

5.2. *Implications*

The predominance of the brand personality variable in determinants of the consideration of CLBPs challenges previous notions, such as perceived benefits usually being regarded as the most important factor in judgments of preference or choice (Lefkoff-Hagius and Mason, 1993). Despite the fact that numerous researchers have demonstrated a significant and positive relation between the perceived benefit and consumer decision-making (e.g., Bove and Johnson, 2000; Mai and Ness, 1997; Cho *et al.*, 2002), this research highlights the critical role played by the perceived brand personality, and further suggests researchers and practitioners should take into account the consumer perceived brand personality when they examine consumer behaviour in relation to brands.

In terms of curbing counterfeits, emphasizing image benefits related to BPs over their counterparts CLBPs might not achieve such good results as stressing brand personality differentiation between these two versions of one brand. As "typical user, brand endorsers, company employees, and the CEO of the company" are the direct influential factors on the consumer perceived brand personality (Aaker, 1997), marketing campaigns might therefore gain remarkable success if they were set up around the themes of differences between the typical user, brand endorsers, company employees, and the CEOs of the companies of the BPs and the CLBPs.

The research finding suggests that the more consumers believe the CLBPs are disposable, the more likely they will buy them. This finding recommends that consumers' consumption notions might have changed significantly in relation to some products. "Long-lasting" is not consumers' concern relating to consideration of the CLBPs. Contrary to conventional thought which suggests that emphasizing the "sub-quality" nature of counterfeits will discourage consumers from purchasing counterfeits, the research highlights that the commonly adopted conventional means might result in a reverse outcome. Nevertheless, this implication should be viewed with caution, as it might not be applicable to all products.

The research findings recommend that demographic variables do not appear to have a significant effect on consumers' likelihood of consideration of CLBPs. In contrast to Wee *et al.* (1995), who suggest segmentation of consumers according to their demographic profiles, the results of this research imply demographic variables should not be used to segment consumers in study of consumer behaviour concerning counterfeits.

5.3. *Limitations*

The results of this research must be taken in the light of some limitations. The present study is exploratory in nature, and to some extent lacks the sophistication and statistical rigours found in most confirmatory types of research. For instance, a convenience sample was used rather than a probability sample. Although great effort was made to minimise drawbacks concerning use of a nonprobability sampling method, the researcher is nevertheless still not entirely confident in claiming that the sampling method adopted is better theoretically than probability sampling. As such, generalisability to the whole population of consumers may be limited to some extent.

Only one version of CLBP of each tested brand was used as stimulus in the current research. In reality, the tested BPs might have a range of counterfeit versions (Gentry *et al.*, 2001) available in the market place. The perceived brand image of these counterfeit versions might be distinguishable from each other even in the context of nondeceptive counterfeiting. Therefore, the research findings should be viewed with caution. More specifically, they might only be applicable to the counterfeit versions appearing in flea markets but not the ones sold in shopping malls, which are more likely to be better quality and higher price versions of counterfeits (Gentry *et al.*, 2001).

Purchasing counterfeits is considered as morally unacceptable and even as supporting organised crime. These research data are based on consumers' self-reports, which means that the data collected could be influenced by the respondents' attempts to produce more socially acceptable responses. Consequently, there is a possibility that the data collected might be biased to a certain degree, despite the fact that a number of devices were adopted in this research (use of neutral language, clarification of the academic use of the data at the beginning of the questionnaire, displaying the figure that one-third of UK consumers knowingly purchase counterfeits) to minimise the possibility of bias.

5.4. *Further research*

The empirical model would be a more sophisticated and more complex one, in which self-image construct is taken into consideration explicitly. Specifically, self-image might play a moderating role in the consideration models. Similarly, later researchers could extend the current research by examining the moderating role of the self-assessed product knowledge on consumer choice processes. Alternatively, they could also investigate the impact of the objective product knowledge on consumer behaviour in nondeceptive counterfeiting. This would reveal whether heavy users would behave in the same way as light users of a particular brand/product when facing the choice of counterfeits.

Future research could test more brands (say, around ten brands in one product category), including BPs, using both similarity judgment and attribute-based multidimensional scaling techniques to explore where CLBPs and BPs are located in the spatial map. This is consistent with Malhotra (1999), who suggests that eight brands or stimuli should be included to obtain a well-defined spatial map. Direct similarity judgment may be used for obtaining the spatial map, and attribute ratings may be used as an aid to interpret the dimensions of the perceptual map. Similar procedures can be used for preference data. These efforts will assist marketers in obtaining a clear view as to where their BPs stand in the market place when the CLBPs exist.

The current research only investigates the determinants of the consideration set in the context of nondeceptive counterfeiting from the brand image level. It is still not quite clear whether the BP brand image is affected or not after the entry of CLBPs. To achieve this, a before–after experimental design with control would enable researchers to observe the potential change in brand image as a result of the entry of CLBPs. This type of design has been used by a number of previous studies in the study of brand extension (e.g., Diamantopoulos *et al.*, 2005; Morrin, 1999) due to its high level of control in accounting for extraneous factors which can assist in enhancing the internal validity of the research (Calder *et al.*, 1981).

Appendix

Items consumers used to value studied CLBP.

No	Counterfeit Burberry	Counterfeit Louis Vuitton
1	Size	Size
2	Price	Price
3	Material	Material
4	Style	Style
5	Color	Color
6	Practicality	Practicality
7	High quality	High quality
8	Image benefit	Image benefit
9	Fun	Fun
10	Price and quality	Price and quality
11	Value for money (status)	Value for money (status)
12	Disposability	Disposability
13	Exclusivity	Exclusivity
14	Attention attracting	Attention attracting
15	Long last	Prestige
16	Down to earth	Long last
17	Original	Fashionable
18	Unique	Trendy
19	Contemporary	Contemporary
20	Reliable	Successful
21	Corporate	Upper class
22	Successful	Feminine
23	Feminine	Smooth
24	Outdoorsy	Social risk
25	Social risk	Financial risk
26	Financial risk	Psychological risk
27	Psychological risk	

References

Aaker, DA (1996). *Building Strong Brands*. New York: The Free Press.

Aaker, DA, R Batra and JG Myers (1992). *Advertising Management* 4th Ed. Englewood Cliffs, NJ: Prentice-Hall.

Aaker, JL (1997). Dimensions of brand personality. *Journal of Marketing Research*, 34(August), 347–356.

Aaker, JL (1999). The malleable self: The role of self-expression in persuasion. *Journal of Marketing Research*, 36(1), 45–57.

Albers-Miller, N (1999). Consumer misbehavior: Why people buy illicit goods. *Journal of Consumer Marketing*, 16(3), 273–287.

Ang, S, P Cheng, E Lim and S Tambyah (2001). Spot the difference: Consumer responses towards counterfeits. *Journal of Consumer Marketing*, 18(3), 219–235.

Anti-Counterfeiting Group Survey Report (2004). *Why Should You Care about Counterfeiting* [online]. http://www.a-cg.com/guest_frames.html [11 September 2006].

Axelrod, JN (1968). Attitude measures that predict purchase. *Journal of Advertising Research*, 8(1), 3–17.

Bamossy, G and D Scammon (1985). Product counterfeiting: Consumers and manufacturers beware. *Advances in Consumer Research*, 12(1), 334–340.

Batra, R, DR Lehmann and D Singh (1993). The brand personality component of brand goodwill: Some antecedents and consequences. In *Brand Equity and Advertising: Advertising's Role in Building Strong Brands*, DA Aaker and A Biel (eds.), pp. 83–97. Hillsdale, NJ: Lawrence Erlbaum Associates.

Bauer, RA (1960). Consumer behaviour as risk taking. In *Dynamic Marketing for a Changing World*, RS Hancock (ed.), pp. 389–398. Chicago: American Marketing Association.

Belch, HW and MA Belch (1995). *Introduction to Advertising and Promotion: An Integrated Marketing Communications Perspective*, (3rd Ed). Boston, MA: Irwin.

Bian, X and C Veloutsou (2004). Perceived risk when purchasing nondeceptive counterfeit products. Paper presented at the *33rd European Marketing Academia Conference*, Spain.

Bian, X (2006). An examination of factors influencing the formation of the consideration set and consumer purchase intention in the context of non-deceptive counterfeiting. Unpublished PhD Thesis, University of Glasgow, UK.

Bian, X and C Veloutsou (2007). Consumer's attitudes regarding non-deceptive counterfeit brands in the UK and China. *Journal of Brand Management*, 14(3), 211–222.

Biel, A (1993). Converting image into equity. In *Brand Equity and Advertising*, DA Aaker and A Biel (eds.), pp. 67–82. Hillsdale, NJ: Lawrence Erlbaum Associates.

Bloch, P, R Bush and L Campbell (1993). Consumer 'accomplices' in product counterfeiting. *Journal of Consumer Marketing*, 10(4), 27–36.

Bove, LL and LW Johnson (2000). A customer-service worker relationship model. *International Journal Service Industry Management*, 11(5), 491–511.

Brooker, G (1984). An assessment of an expanded measure of perceived risk. *Advances in Consumer Research*, 11(1), 439–441.

Calder, BJ, LW Phillips and AM Tybout (1981). Designing research for application. *Journal of Consumer Research*, 8(9), 197–207.

Campbell, M and R Goodstein (2001). The moderating effect of perceived risk on consumers' evaluation of product incongruity: Preference for the norm. *Journal of Consumer Research*, 28(3), 439–449.

Caruso, JC and N Cliff (1998). The *factor* structure of the WAIS-R: Replicability across age-groups. *Multivariate Behavioral Research*, 33(2), 273–293.

Chakraborty, G, A Allred, AS Sukhdial and T Bristol (1997). Use of negative cues to reduce demand for counterfeit products. *Advances in Consumer Research*, 24(1), 345–349.

Chakraborty, G, A Allred and T Bristol (1996). Exploring consumers' evaluations of counterfeits: The roles of country of origin and ethnocentrism. *Advances in Consumer Research*, 23(1), 379–384.

Chaudhry, PE and MG Walsh (1996). An assessment of the impact of counterfeiting in international markets: The piracy paradox persists. *Columbia Journal of World Business*, 31(3): 34–49.

Cho, Y, I Im, R Hiltz and J Fjermestad (2002). The effects of post-purchase evaluation factors on online vs. offline customer complaining behavior: Implications for customer loyalty. *Advances in Consumer Research*, 29(1), 318–326.

Churchill, GA (1999). *Marketing Research: Methodological Foundations* 7th Ed. London: The Dryden Press.

Cohen, L (1966). The level of consciousness: A dynamic approach to the recall technique. *Journal of Marketing Research*, 3(2), 142–148.

Cordell, V, N Wongtada and L Kieschnick (1996). Counterfeit purchase intentions: Role of lawfulness attitudes and product traits as determinants. *Journal of Business Research*, 35(1), 41–53.

Cordell, V and N Wongtada (1991). Consumer responses to counterfeit products. In T Childers (ed.), *Marketing Theory and Application*, pp. 247.

Cox, DF (ed.) (1967). *Risk Raking and Information Handling in Consumer Behavior*. Boston, MA: Division of Research, Graduate School of Business Administration, Harvard University.

Cunningham, SM (1967). The major dimensions of perceived risk. In *Risk Taking and Information Handling in Consumer Behavior*, DF Cox (ed.), pp. 82–108. Boston, MA: Division of Research, Graduate School of Business Administration, Harvey University.

de Chernatony, L (1993). Categorizing brands: Evolutionary processes underpined by two key dimensions. *Journal of Marketing Management*, 9(2), 173–188.

de Chernatony, L and MHB McDonald (1998). *Creating Powerful Brands in Consumer, Service and Industrial Markets*. Oxford: Butterworth-Heinemann.

Diamantopoulos, A, G Smith and I Grime (2005). The impact of brand extensions on brand personality: Experimental evidence. *European Journal of Marketing*, 39(1/2), 129–149.

Dodge, HR, EA Edwards and S Fullerton (1996). Consumer transgressions in the marketplace: Consumers' perspectives. *Psychology & Marketing*, 13(8), 821–835.

Dolich, IJ (1969). Congruence relationships between self images and product brands. *Journal of Marketing Research*, 6(1), 80–84.

Erdem, T and J Swait (1998). Brand equity as a signaling phenomenon. *Journal of Consumer Psychology*, 7(2), 131–157.

Fishbein, M (1967). Attitude and the prediction of behavior. In *Attitude Theory and Measurement*, M Fishbein (ed.), pp. 477–492. New York: Wiley.

Freedman, H (1999). Chinese copycat are leaving international brands fit to be tied. *Forbes*, 163, 48–54.

Freling, T and L Forbes (2005). An examination of brand personality through methodological triangulation. *Journal of Brand Management*, 13(2), 148–162.

Gabbott, M (1991). The role of product cues in assessing risk in second-hand markets. *European Journal of Marketing*, 25(9), 38–50.

Gentry, JW, S Putrevu, CJ Shultz and S Commuri (2001). How now Ralph Lauren? The separation of brand and product in a counterfeit culture. *Advances in Consumer Research*, 27(1), 258–265.

Gentury, JW, S Putrevu and CJ Shultz (2006). The effects of counterfeiting on consumer search, *Journal of Consumer Behavior*, 5, 245–256.

Grossman, G and C Shapiro (1988a). Foreign counterfeiting of status goods. *Journal of Economics*, 103(1), 79–100.

Grossman, G and C Shapiro (1988b). Counterfeit-product trade. *American Economic Review*, 78(1), 59–75.

Harvey, MG and IA Ronkainen (1985). International counterfeiters: Marketing success without the cost and the risk. *Columbia Journal of World Business*, 20(3), 37–45.

Harvey, PJ and WD Walls (2003). The revealed demand for pirate goods: Probit analysis of experimental data. *International Journal of Management*, 20(2), 194–201.

Hem, LE and NM Iversen (2002). Decomposed similarity measures in brand extensions. *Advances in Consumer Research*, 29(1), 199–206.

Hinkin, T (1995). A review of scale development practices in the study of organisations. *Journal of Management*, 21(5), 967–968.

Hoe, L, G Hogg and S Hart (2003). Fakin it: Counterfeiting and consumer contradictions. *Proceedings of European Advances in Consumer Research*, Vol. 6.

Holden, SJS (1993). Understanding brand awareness: Let me give you a c(lue). *Advances in Consumer Research*, 20(1), 383–388.

Hopkins, D, L Kontnik and M Trunage (2003). *Counterfeiting Exposed-Protecting Your Brand and Customers*. New York, USA: Wiley.

Hornik, J (1982). Impact of pre-call request form and gender interaction on response to the mail survey. *Journal of Marketing Research*, 19(1), 144–151.

Hornik, J and S Ellis (1988). Strategies to secure compliance for a mall intercept interview. *Public Opinion Quarterly*, 52(4), 539–551.

Jacoby, J and L Kaplan (1972). The components of perceived risk. In *Proceedings of the 3rd Annual Conference Chicago*.

Johar, J and M Sirgy (1991). Value-expressive versus utilitarian advertising appeals: When and who use which appeal. *Journal of Advertising*, 20(3), 23–33.

Johnson, MD and CP Puto (1987). A review of consumer judgement and choice. In *Review of Marketing*, M Houston (ed.), pp. 236–292. USA: American Marketing Association.

Kaiser, HF (1974). An index of factorial simplicity. *Psychometrika*, 39(1), 31–36.

Kapferer, J-N (1995). Brand confusion: Empirical study of a legal concept. *Psychology & Marketing*, 12(6), 551–569.

Keller, KL (1993). Conceptualizing, measuring, and managing consumer-based brand equity. *Journal of Marketing*, 57(1), 1–22.

Kleine, RE, SS Klein and JB Kernan (1993). Mundane consumption and the self: A social-identity perspective. *Journal of Consumer Research*, 3(3), 327–343.

Kotler, P (1999). *Marketing management: Analysis, planning, implementation, and control.* New Jersey: Prentice-Hall.

Lefkoff-Hagius, R and C Mason (1993). Characteristics, beneficial, and image attributes in consumer judgements of similarity and preference. *Journal of Consumer Research*, 20(1), 100–110.

Mai, L-W and M Ness (1997). Consumers' perceptions of mail-order speciality foods. *Journal of Marketing Management*, 13(7), 705–724.

Malhotra, NK (1988). Self concept and product choice: An integrated perspective. *Journal of Economic Psychology*, 9(1), 1–28.

Malhotra, NK (1999). *Marketing research: An applied orientation.* 3rd Ed. London: Prentice-Hall International.

Mandel, N (2003). Shifting selves and decision making: The effects of self-construal priming on consumer risk-taking. *Journal of Consumer Research*, 30(1), 30–40.

Mitchell, V-W and P Boustani (1993). Market development using new products and new customers: A role for perceived risk. *European Journal of Marketing*, 27(2), 17–32.

Mitchell, V-W (1999). Consumer perceived risk: Conceptualisations and models. *European Journal of Marketing*, 33(1/2), 163–195.

Morrin, M (1999). The impact of brand extensions on parent brand memory structures and retrieval processes. *Journal of Marketing Research*, 36(4), 517–525.

Mowen, JC (1993). *Consumer Behavior*, 3rd Ed. New York: Macmillan Publishing Company.

Myers, J and A Shocker (1981). The nature of product-related attributes. In *Research in Marketing*, J Sheth (ed.), Vol. 5, pp. 211–236. Greenwich CT: JAI Press.

Nedungadi, P (1990). Recall and consumer consideration sets: Influencing choice without altering brand evaluation. *Journal of Consumer Research*, 17(3), 263–276.

Nia, A and J Zaichowsky (2000). Do counterfeit devalue the ownership of luxury brands? *Journal of Product and Brand Management*, 9(7), 485–497.

Nowell, C and LR Stanley (1991). Length-biased sampling in mall intercept surveys. *Journal of Marketing Research*, 28(4), 475–479.

Penz, E and B Stöttinger (May 2003). Brands and counterfeits — What do they have in common? Paper presented at the *European Marketing Academy Conference*, UK.

Penz, E and B Stöttinger (2005). Forget the "Real" thing-take the copy! An explanatory model for the volitional purchase of counterfeit products. *Advances in Consumer Research*, 32(1), 568–575.

Perrier R (ed.) (1997). *Brand Valuation.* London: Premier Books.

Peter, PJ and JC Olson (1994). *Understanding Consumer Behavior.* Burr Ridge, IL: McGraw-Hill/Irwin.

Phau, I, G Prendergast and LH Chuen (2001). Profiling brand-piracy-prone consumers: An exploratory study in Hong Kong's clothing industry. *Journal of Fashion Marketing and Management*, 5(1), 45–55.

Plummer, JT (1985). How personality makes a difference. *Journal of Advertising Research*, 24(6), 27–31.

Plummer, JT (2000). How personality makes a difference. *Journal of Advertising Research*, 40(6), 79–83.

Poulter, S (28 April 2006). Cheap and chic fakes snapped up by the smart set. *Daily Mail*, p. 28.

Preacher, KJ and RC MacCallum (2003). Repairing Tom Swift's electric factor analysis machine. *Understanding Statistics*, 2(1), 13–43.

Puth, G, P Mostert and M Ewing (1999). Consumer perceptions of mentioned product and brand attributes in magazine advertising. *Journal of Product & Brand Management*, 8(1), 38–49.

Rao, AR, L Qu and RW Ruekert (1999). Signaling unobservable product quality through a brand ally. *Journal of Marketing Research*, 36 (May), 258–268.

Romaniuk, J (2003). Brand attributes — "Distribution outlets" in the mind. *Journal of Marketing Communications*, 9(2), 73–92.

Roselius, T (1971). Consumer rankings of risk reduction methods. *Journal of Marketing*, 35(1), 56–61.

Salzer-Mörling, M (2004). Silence of the brands. *European Journal of Marketing*, 38(1/2), 224–238.

Shultz, II CJ and B Saporito (1996). Protecting intellectual property: Strategies and recommendations to deter counterfeiting and brand piracy in global markets. *The Columbia Journal of World Business*, 31(1), 18–28.

Sirgy, J (1982). Self-concept in consumer behavior: A critical review. *Journal of Consumer Research*, 9(3), 287–300.

Stokmans, M (1991). The relative importance of product attributes: Consumer decision theories in new-product development. Published Doctorial Dissertation, Delft University Press, Delft.

Tom, G, B Garibaldi, Y Zeng and J Pilcher (1998). Consumer demand for counterfeit goods. *Psychology & Marketing*, 15(5), 405–421.

Troye, S (1983). Evoke set formation from the perspective of decision making as an instance of categorization. Unpublished PhD thesis, University of Illinois at Urbana-Champaign, Illinois.

Wee, C, S-J Tan and K-H Cheok (1995). Non-price determinants of intention to purchase counterfeit goods. *International Marketing Review*, 12(6), 19–47.

DOCTORAL RESEARCH NOTES

6

MATERIALISM IN EUROPE: A CROSS-CULTURAL APPROACH

Fernando Augusto de Sá Neves dos Santos*

Instituto Politécnico da Guarda, Portugal

Elizabeth Reis

Department of Quantitative Methods, ISCTE Business School, Lisbon, Portugal

The main objective of this chapter is to examine the invariance of Richins and Dawson's (1992) previously validated three-factor materialism model scale across different cultural groups of respondents and to analyse and estimate the presence of materialistic values among Europeans, more precisely in samples from Germany, Spain, and Portugal. Through Richins and Dawson's (1992) materialism values scale, we checked and cross-examined the materialistic dimensions among the young people of the countries referred to using Structural Equation Modeling. There are different levels and sort of materialism among the three European countries.

Keywords: Materialism; Germany; Spain; Portugal; structural equation models (SEM).

1. Introduction

Paleo-archaeologist theories have always affirmed that material objects helped to make us human (Childe, 1936 cited by Wallendorf and Arnould, 1988). The different roles the material objects represent in our lives have transformed a lot of goods into primary basic needs in present-day life. Increasingly, the contemporary developmental process decisively brings

---

*Corresponding author.

especially young people face to face with the need to consume: "*Grandir, c'est consommer*" (Brée, 1993, p. 111). The influence of advertising, life circumstances, the increasing number of divorces, and single parents as well as the need for two working parents are all factors which lead to more child involvement in the shopping, making consumption increasingly common for young people (Graham and Hamdan, 1987). The search for happiness through consumption and purchasing now has an increasingly relevant role in Western societies (Ger and Belk, 1996).

The entertainment and advertising roles of the media interfere in the rituals of society (Otnes and Scott, 1996) to create desirable lifestyles. Even if they do not correspond entirely to reality, these images are created to raise audience expectations (Englis and Solomon, 1995). Consumer behaviour reflects the influences of these messages and images of success, especially on television, altering their satisfaction, motivation, and desires (O'Guinn and Shrum, 1997). The values and idealised lifestyle patterns that are broadcast can influence and modify one's perception of reality (Gerbner *et al.*, 1980).

To Hofstede (1997), people's procedures and attitudes are a result of principles and values taught by the groups in their environment. These values establish people's patterns of thought, behaviour, and attitudes as well as their consumer behaviour (Roberts, 1998). Materialistic behaviour, is derived from factors related to one's environment, communication with family and peers, mass media, and the appeal of popular trendsetters (Clark *et al.*, 2001), but is also related to the ease of acquisition of more and more products that provide well-being or satisfaction of needs (Twitchell, 2000).

Most of the empirical research investigating materialism uses US samples to develop and validate the measuring instrument. The applicability of these measures in other cultures must be tested and cross-cultural properties of measures verified (dimension and reliability) (Douglas and Craig, 1983). The purpose of this work is to examine the invariance of the previously validated three-factor materialism scale proposed by Richins and Dawson (1992) across different cultural groups of respondents and to reveal the level of materialism in young people from several European countries — Portugal, Spain, and Germany.

2. Materialism

Consumer behaviour is a result of various influences that all individuals are exposed to during their growing and learning process as well as a result of knowledge and information transmitted by all groups, by personal experience

(Sproles and Sproles, 1990; Walsh *et al.*, 2001), information, education, and family communication (Alsop, 1988; Rindfleisch *et al.*, 1997) or by the media (Carlson *et al.*, 1990). Images of success transmitted by the media make consumers want to become those images of success by acquiring a great number of specific material goods (Englis and Solomon, 1995; Englis *et al.*, 1993; O'Guinn and Shrum, 1997). To Rindfleisch *et al.* (1997), family disruption can influence materialistic attitudes by promoting consumption responsibilities in children and also by the demonstration of affection made through gifts that characterises divorced parents.

The word "value" is understood by economists as the cost or price of one object but to sociologists and marketers, it is the benefit given to an individual by a good or the property that classifies an object or a product as desirable and loved (Richins, 1994). The social interpretation of this concept can be defined as the principle that guides the way an individual or collectivity acts or behaves according to a recognised social ideal (Kamakura and Novak, 1992). Values of each society (Zhang and Gelb, 1996; Rose, 1999), transmitted over generations through communication, education and scholarship, or through socialisation, make people more materialistic, defining their lives by the possession and acquisition of more and more objects (Richins, 1994). Young people concentrate on getting more objects that give them a sensation of success and happiness (Richins and Dawson, 1992). Economic growth itself encourages consumption or desire for material goods, making the purchase a sought-after moment of pleasure.

Social theory sustains the popular concept of materialism that all consumers have (Fournier and Richins, 1991), based on the value objects have for individuals and the role they play in their lives, associated with feelings of possession, happiness, and social status. Materialism became part of human condition (Abela, 2006), despite each individual assuming attitudes and behaviours that are differentiated from others. The research in materialism suggests that people who emphasise acquisition and possession of material objects are materialistic while those who do not feel this need are not materialistic (Belk, 1985; Richins and Dawson, 1992; Richins, 1994). These materialistic feelings are present in all societies and cultures; differences exist only in what different individuals value and aspire to because there are also differences in what is considered important by society (Hofstede, 1997).

It is known that material goods play an important role in the life of each individual. To anthropologists, an individual acquires habits and pleasures whose systematic satisfaction becomes a basic need. Attachment to objects is not due to monetary value but rather to the expressions of self-concept, feelings, memories and the sense of security provided, and the connection to others (Wallendorf and Arnould, 1988).

There are several definitions of materialism. Belk (1985) defines materialism as the importance the consumer gives to his/her worldly possessions. People who present higher levels of materialism place possessions at the centre of their lives as the main source of satisfaction or dissatisfaction. Ward and Wackman (1971) describe materialism as the tendency to find the fundamental elements to reach personal happiness and social progress in material goods and money. Mukerji (1983, p. 8) refers to materialism as "*a cultural system in which material interests are not made subservient to other social goals*"; instead, interest in material things is the most important focus in that culture or society. Richins and Dawson (1992) define materialism as the value that possessions represent in individuals' lives which regulates the quantity and quality of their purchases. To Browne and Kaldenberg (1997), materialism is a combination of attitudes, values, and sentiments associated with possessions that guide one's selection of events and objects.

The concept of materialism has shown the importance in consumer behaviour when connected to compulsive shopping or with the change of consumer patterns valorising possessions (Richins, 1994). Materialism also has influence on the principles or values that guide people's lives, either by ethic values that determine their attitudes (Muncy and Eastman, 1998), or the valorisation of material objects as the way to reach happiness and social progress (Ward and Wackman, 1971). The role and the value of objects are connected to the need for and pursuit of possessions to achieve happiness, success, and social status (Belk, 1985).

3.   Literature Review and Materialism Scales

Many articles and studies attempt to address the effects and consequences of materialism on society, just as others try to develop scales that will quantify the level of materialism and how it influences individual behaviour. Richins and Dawson (1992) mention one of the first studies in 1957 by Dickins and Ferguson to measure materialism in children, and another from 1969 by Campbell that measured materialistic attitudes. Subsequent studies have developed new measuring instruments for materialism or materialistic attitudes. Among more recent studies, Belk's (1985) research stands out. This study infers measures about personality traits. The next instrument to measure materialism attitudes was validated by Richins and Dawson's (1992) research, on their 18-item scale with three subscales.

Meanwhile, several studies analysed the relationship between materialism and variables connected with consumer behaviour. Those studies were centred in demographic and psychological individuals characteristics, which confirmed and contradicted conclusions of previous studies.

Dittmar and Pepper (1994) applied the Richins and Dawson (1992) measure scale to a British sample and concluded by the weak impact of materialistic values in person perceptions but moderated the strength with sociocultural representations about wealth and poverty are reproduced. Richins (1994) concludes that the higher materialistic individuals judged others by their possessions and valorised more public consumed products, meanwhile the less materialistic give more attentions to relations valuing the goods associated to personal and family relations. For Ger and Belk (1996), materialism is consumption oriented to the demand of happiness and represent a materialism culture trait that influences and affect shopping behaviour (O'Guinn and Faber, 1989; Mick, 1996).

Rindfleirch *et al.* (1997) analyse the relationship between family structure and compulsive consumption that are connected to the resources available, family stress and satisfaction of life that influences the consumer behaviour. Roberts *et al.* (2003, 2006) conclude the same, that family structure is related to the level of materialism and compulsive buying of young adults. The young adults who have grown up in a disrupted familial ambience find in material possessions a sort of security and sense of happiness. Autonomy consented by divorced parents promote opportunities to substitute personal relations by material possessions and that affects the child's life and attitudes until advanced age (30 years), associating materialism to success and place possessions at the centre of their lives (Roberts *et al.*, 2006).

To Browne and Kaldenberg (1997) higher materialistic individuals tend to buy products that transmit their image among others. Webster and Beatty (1997) have found Thailand's consumers give significantly more importance to the success materialism dimension than North-Americans. Bachman (1997) analyse materialism attitudes between North-Americans and conclude these do not change with age. Chan (2006a) concluded older Chinese children, between 6 and 12 years, associated material possessions with waste and the younger children to happiness, friendship, and self-esteem. Chan (2006b) also concluded that older children are more materialistic and tend to communicate more with their peers and less with their parents.

To Chang and Arkin (2002) materialism is connected to personal uncertainty and uncertainty relating to society, is negatively related with self-esteem and life satisfaction and positively related to society anxiety and public consciousness. Wang and Wallendorf (2006) conclude the same negative relationship between materialism and satisfaction with higher social status products.

Christopher *et al.* (2005) have analysed the relationship between materialism and the individual self-presentational style. They conclude the higher materialistic individuals are more insecure and present low self-esteem avoidance by using supplication or ingratiation to hide weakness or helplessness. The results also indicate that materialistic individual's do not use intimidation or self-promotion beyond others.

Kilbourne *et al.* (2005) find that for Germany, Canada, and US individuals that there is a positive relationship between materialism and self-enhancement and negative relationship with self-transcendence.

Several studies confirmed the value of the 18-item scale: Richins (1994), Mick (1996), Rindfleirch *et al.* (1997), Bachman (1997), Browne and Kaldenberg (1997) with an US sample. Other studies used the scale in cross-cultural investigation, Ditmar and Pepper (1994) with a Great Britain sample, Webster and Beatty (1997) with samples from the United States and Thailand, and Eastman *et al.* (1997) with samples from the United States, China, and Mexico.

Richins and Dawson (1992) propose that needs, emotions, or personal desires with other purposes beyond possession support the acquisition process. They verified the existence of three personality traits, individual feelings, or materialistic dimensions that make up the set of individual values that condition behaviour and are directly correlated to the materialism concept. First, *Centrality in Acquisition* represents the express will of accumulating material goods. To Richins and Dawson, acquiring goods is the way to obtain a greater level of consumption; it is a lifestyle for materialistic individuals, in whose life possession and acquisition is the main objective.

Individuals who see possession and acquisition as essential to reach happiness, satisfaction, and well-being help to define the second dimension of Richins and Dawson materialism scale. *Acquisition as the pursuit of happiness* is an orientation that does not distinguish social progress, well-being, or happiness from material possessions.

The third dimension identified by the authors considers that materialistic individuals "... judge their own and others' success by the number and quality of possessions accumulated" (Richins and Dawson, 1992, p. 304). Both the quality and quantity of material things possessed by individuals confer status and project identity or successful images (Campbell, 1987; Rassuli and Hollander, 1986). Thus, *possession-defined success* leads individuals to cherish goods for their cost and quantity rather than the satisfaction they yield.

To establish generality of materialistic values, Richins and Dawson's (1992) scale must be administered to other populations. To guarantee comparability values among different cultures, other studies in different cultures must be carried out (Leung and Bond, 1989; Triandis, 1972). The main objective of this study is: to establish evidence of the level of materialism in young people from Germany, Spain, and Portugal; to evaluate the relative differences in three dimensions in these countries; to compare behaviour differences between materialistic and nonmaterialistic individuals; and, finally, to compare these materialistic values with American young adults.

4. Methodology

All consumers present some level of materialism, albeit with differences in each dimension and in each individual (Fournier and Richins, 1991). Each country has particular values and cultural patterns (Hofstede, 1997), which is why differences should be found in attitudes and in the comprehension of the same events by individuals from different countries. Resemblances among cultures can lead to valid measures and concepts that allow the comparison of values, attitudes, and pattern behaviour (Steenkamp and Baumgartner, 1998). Culture measures can be looked at from two perspectives: the *emic*, whereby there are specific measures to each culture, or the *etic* vision, which looks to find valid measures in different cultural environments (Douglas and Craig, 1983).

Different social values lead to individuals with diverse ideals and life goals. To understand the different materialistic attitudes in different cultures, the applicability of value scales in other countries and cultures must be tested. For this study, the data, collected in Portugal, Spain, and Germany, were obtained through the answers to 18 items of Richins and Dawson's (1992) materialistic value scale (a 5-level Likert scale, from strongly agree to strongly disagree). The samples comprised young people aged 18 to 25, mainly university students, because using a more homogeneous group would minimise random error (Durvasula *et al.*, 1993). A total of 1037 students participated in the study: 500 from Portugal, 330 from Spain, and 207 from Germany. The original scale in English was translated into the languages of the three countries involved. To ensure the meaning, thought, and concept of each questionnaire item remained unchanged, the instrument was translated from English to each of the languages and then translated back to English.

To analyse the data cross-culturally, the principles proposed by literature (Leung and Bond, 1989) were followed, using intra- and cross-cultural analysis. Cross-cultural analysis is predicated on invariant scale measures while the national, or intracultural, analysis examines the more appropriate models for each country. The multigroup structural equation models (SEM) reveal the presence of invariant patterns between countries to permit comparison among them (Myers *et al.*, 2000). Multivariate statistical procedures are used in cross-cultural analysis for assessing the cross-national applicability of the scales which are consistent with the data.

To evaluate the dimensionality of materialism scale of the data of the countries involved in this study, confirmatory factor analysis was applied using SEM software. Structural equation modelling examines a series of dependent relationships simultaneously to study multiple dependence and interrelatedness between observed indicators and latent variables that should indicate the theoretical relations of the model (Byrne 1998; Salgueiro and Reis 2000) and provide statistical efficiency (Hair *et al.*, 1998). *AMOS 4.0* was used to analyse the covariance and means of the items (the maximum likelihood estimation process was used because it simplifies the test of hypothesis to achieve the goodness of fit model [Arbuckle and Wothke, 1999]).

5. Results

According to Arbuckle and Wothke (1999), various measures can be used to evaluate the adjustment of a model while the specific measures of the model fitting process depend on the researcher. The CMIN or chi-square (χ^2) represents the statistic test of the discrepancy of the sample. Researchers have addressed its limitations, but it is used as a comparison measure between different models (Byrne, 2001). The CMIN/DF ratio is the minimum discrepancy divided by its degrees of freedom. The adequacy of the model is determined by this ratio and should be near 2 and below 5 to indicate a reasonable fit. Goodness-of-fit index (GFI) compares the adjustment of the model to the data, measures the relative amount of variance and covariance of sample data and should be close to 1. The comparative fit index (CFI)

Table 1.   Multiple group analysis of material values scale.

Country	Valid inquiries	CMIN	DF	CMIN/DF	GFI	CFI	TLI	RMSEA
Multi group	998	1193.619	396	3.014	0.878	0.757	0.718	0.045
Portugal	477	485.787	132	3.680	0.893	0.737	0.695	0.075
Spain	319	419.138	132	3.175	0.861	0.782	0.747	0.083
Germany	202	288.518	132	2.186	0.871	0.748	0.708	0.077

provides the measure of complete covariation of data, while the Tucker Lewis coefficient (TLI), another measure of the adjustment, combines the moderation measure or cost effectiveness of the model between the model proposed and the null model. The root mean square error of approximation (RMSEA) expresses the error of approximation to the population, and the value of this index of about 0.05 or less would indicate a close fit of the model in relation to the degrees of freedom.

Findings from a preliminary factorial analysis of Richins and Dawson's (1992) 18 items confirmed the multigroup invariance. Global adjustment indices revealed nonequivalence of the groups as shown in Table 1. The equivalence of model between cultural groups, or configural invariance, was not supported; the index values indicate a lack of fit.

The internal consistency measures in Table 2, of all scale and subscales of material values defined by Richins and Dawson (1992), shows that only two alpha of Cronbach indices (Success subscale in Portugal and Happiness in Germany) were slightly below acceptable level (0.6 is regarded as the minimum necessary value for acceptable scale reliability, Hair *et al.*, 1999).

Then, through exploratory factorial cross-cultural analysis, a new model was found nested to the original to permit comparison of the material values levels of young people (Byrne, 2001). Through the structure analysis of modification indices and regression weights to each country, the analysis and revision of the original modified model verified that:

— Item 12, "I like a lot of luxury in my life," as part of subscale Centrality in Acquisition shares its loading on all three subscales. However,

Table 2.   Alpha de Cronbach to subscales.

Country	Materialism	Success	Centrality	Happiness
Portugal	0.7104	0.5715	0.6484	0.6538
Spain	0.8040	0.6048	0.7445	0.6842
Germany	0.7592	0.6903	0.6170	0.5850

the modification indices for regression weights indicate a cross-loading between the first and the second dimensions in all countries in this study (subscale, Possession-defined Success), indicating good reason to establish a *cross-loading* for this item;

— The loading of Item 9, "The things I own aren't all that important to me," in the second latent variable, is not significant in all groups, so this item was abandoned;

— In the first latent variable, a higher level of correlated errors or misspecification was found associated with the pair of Items 3 and 6, respectively: "I don't place much emphasis on the amount of material objects people own as sign of success," "I don't pay much attention to the material objects other people own". This measurement error covariance represents systematic, rather than random measurement error in item responses, which can result from the fact that these two items essentially ask the same question. Consequently, Item 6 was abandoned.

The analysis of each group in the new model showed a marked improvement in the goodness-of-fit indices (Table 3).

The fully constrained multigroup model was estimated with the nested model and the chi-square value provided the basis of comparison with the previously fitted models. Testing the invariance of this constrained model, the chi-square of the corrected model is significant ($\chi^2 = 772.680$; 300 degrees of freedom), similar to the improvement of the other indices (CMIN/DF = 2.576; GFI = 0.912; CFI = 0.844; TLI = 0.813; RMSEA = 0.04), suggesting an acceptable fit of the three-factor model. The items' loadings are significant in their respective factors ($p < 0.05$). A total of 51 factor-loadings are significant; 71% of standardised loadings exceed 0.4, suggesting the fit of the model to the data. Latent variables present moderate or high correlations: 0.23, 0.34, 0.49 between the first and second subscales; 0.04, 0.24, 0.31 between the second and the third; and 0.41, 0.77, 0.60 between the first and third subscales for Portugal, Spain, and Germany, respectively. Then other models were used to test discriminant validity. The chi-square for a

Table 3. Goodness-of-fit of the material value scale model across countries.

Country	CMIN	DF	CMIN/DF	GFI	CFI	TLI	RMSEA
Portugal	317.964	100	3.180	0.922	0.823	0.788	0.068
Spain	274.343	100	2.743	0.901	0.860	0.832	0.074
Germany	180.275	100	1.803	0.907	0.853	0.824	0.063

single-factor model was compared with chi-square for three-factor model to each country ($\chi^2 = 800.615$ (df = 104); 555.801 (104); 299.477 (104); Portugal, Spain, and Germany, respectively). The difference in chi-square test was significant, indicating a superior fitting in the three-factor model. The same proceedings were used to guarantee the discriminant validity for all the possible two-factor combination models such that all the three-dimensional models present better indices of adjustment to data.

Based on the analysis above, the three-factor model fit the data well cross-nationally, with significant loadings on salient factors and zero loadings on nonsalient factors. It is for the cross-national model or the configural invariance of the model, although it does not imply that consumers in those countries respond to the items in the same way. To conduct comparative analysis of values among countries, the cross-invariance of each measure scale must be shown and the partial equivalence of models must be verified (Byrne, 2001).

The existence of metric invariance demonstrates that the answers can be compared as long as the presence of similar scale intervals for all countries is proven. The equivalence of answers scale permits comparison of the scores of different items which will correspond to dissimilarities between cultures (Steenkamp and Baumgartner, 1998). The next step is to establish factor loadings invariance across countries. Table 4 demonstrates the significant increase in chi-square between the model of configural invariance and the model of full metric invariance ($\Delta\chi^2(28) = 57.034$; $p < 0.05$), even if the fit did not decrease considerably in the alternative fit indices. Inspection of modification indices (MI) reveals that the significant increase in chi-square was due to a lack of invariance or cultural equivalence of several items. The

Table 4. Goodness-of-fit statistic for test of invariance material scale values across countries.

Model multigroups	CMIN	GL	CMIN/DF	GFI	CFI	TLI	RMSEA
Configural invariance	772.680	300	2.576	0.912	0.844	0.813	0.040
Full metric invariance	829.714	328	2.530	0.907	0.834	0.818	0.039
Final partial metric invariance	809.193	324	2.498	0.908	0.840	0.822	0.039
Full factor variance invariance	828.781	330	2.511	0.906	0.835	0.820	0.039
Final partial factor variance invariance	819.419	328	2.498	0.907	0.838	0.822	0.039
Full covariance invariance of factors	853.703	334	2.556	0.903	0.828	0.815	0.040
Final partial covariance invariance of factors	826.744	330	2.505	0.907	0.836	0.821	0.039

test for partial metric invariance (Lastovicka, 1982) was conducted and one after the other of the constraint invariances of the loadings that presented problems or with the largest MI were loosened up. After setting free the loadings of Items 8 and 16, the indices of the model presented an acceptable fit. As presented in Table 5, the chi-square statistics of the fit of the model indicate this model is not significantly worse than the configural invariance model ($\Delta \chi^2(2) = 0.467$; $p > 0.05$; with the other indices almost unchanged, GFI, CFI, RMSEA), supporting partial metric invariance.

The hypothesis of invariance of the variance of factors was tested by constraining all variances to be invariant across countries; the significant differences found ($\Delta \chi^2(6) = 19.588$; $p < 0.01$) helped to determine which variances contribute to this inequality. The variance of Success factor distinguishes the young Germans from the others. Removing the equality constraint to variance of success factor, the model was tested with the invariant variance of only two dimensions and, as demonstrated in Table 5 ($\Delta \chi^2(4) = 10.226$; $p > 0.05$), the chi-square value reveals the existence of equality of variance of Centrality and Happiness dimensions across countries.

To establish factor covariance invariance, another confirmatory factor analysis was performed; the further constraint of factor covariance across countries, as presented in Table 4 ($\Delta \chi^2(6) = 34.284$; $p < 0.01$), demonstrates model weakness. The analysis of MI shows nonequivalent covariance of Happiness across countries; the relaxing of this covariance constraint supports partial covariance invariance of factors ($\Delta \chi^2(2) = 7.325$; $p > 0.05$).

We can conclude that the materialistic value scale is well-defined through a three-factor model — Success, Centrality, and Happiness — associated to shopping behaviour of Portuguese, Spanish and German young people, although different cultures present different relations to these factors. Despite the equivalence in some observed variables in the three countries, there are differences in the structural relations between materialistic values. There are also significant differences in the way that the different groups evaluate Success and, consequently, the equality of the variance of this dimension is not

Table 5. Construct reliability to subscales of material values.

	Success	Centrality	Happiness
Portugal	0.619	0.681	0.659
Spain	0.690	0.728	0.692
Germany	0.701	0.616	0.608

verified. Similarly, differences were found in the Happiness and Centrality dimensions as well as between Happiness and Success.

The Construct Reliability[1] (Hair *et al.* 1998, p. 624) (Table 5) with the reversed items of negative loadings, shows that the material subscales are reliable (> 0.6) in the three countries.

The model equivalence structure and the loadings of materialistic values across groups permits analysis of the mean differences of latent variables (Marsh *et al.*, 2002). To compare mean factors, scalar equivalence of items is determined through the equivalence of intercepts or the equivalence of the constant term of observed variables equation. Given that only partial metric invariance was achieved, only the intercepts of invariant factors were constrained to be equal across countries. The increase of chi-square between the model of scalar equivalence ($\chi^2 = 1254.600$; df = 346) and the partial metric invariance model is highly significant, but the improvement of the other indices suggest an adequate fit of the model (TLI = 0.970; CFI = 0.975; RMSEA = 0.051). These results provide mixed support for the scalar invariance model and imply that the difference of scores on scales can be meaningfully compared across countries (Li *et al.*, 1996; Steenkamp and Baumgartner, 1998).

Table 6 presents the item loadings of the final model of each country. Tables 6 and 7 indicate that materialism values are different across countries. To Portuguese young people, the need to acquire and possession is related to their goal of achieving Happiness. Young students from Spain and Germany focus on possession and the accumulation of goods, with higher levels of Centrality in acquisition. Germans have the higher mean of materialism connected to acquisition, accumulation, and the Success dimension. For Portuguese and Spanish young people, Happiness is more important than Success with respect to materialism, which differentiated them from Germans.

6. Comparison of Materialism Values

To identify if the means differences to each subscale are significant across groups, tests must be carried out on the differences of means among the countries, comparing the chi-square adjustment values of each model to consider the equivalence of means (Durvasula *et al.*, 2001). For example, this can be

---

[1] Construct reliability

$$= \frac{(\text{Sum of standardised loadings})^2}{(\text{Sum of standardised loadings})^2 + \text{Sum of indicator of measurement error}}$$

Table 6.   Subscales and items of material values (base model: partial scalar invariance).

Subscales	Portugal	Spain	Germany
Success			
I admire people who own expensive homes, cars and clothes	0.638	0.713	0.670
Some of the most important achievements in life include acquiring material possessions	0.424	0.503	0.539
I don't place much emphasis on the amount of material objects people own as sign of success[a]	0.249	0.268	0.304
The things I own say a lot about how well I'm doing in life	0.396	0.495	0.452
I like to own things that impress people	0.525	0.601	0.561
I like a lot of luxury in my life	0.437	0.519	0.494
Centrality			
I usually buy only the things I need[a]	0.753	0.781	0.598
I try to keep my life simple, as far as possessions concerned[a]	0.676	0.726	0.742
I enjoy spending money on things that aren't practical	0.552	0.603	0.463
Buying things gives me a lot of pleasure	0.388	0.373	0.310
I like a lot of luxury in my life	0.303	0.314	0.239
I put less emphasis on material things than most people I know[a]	0.307	0.313	0.254
Happiness			
I have all the things I really need to enjoy life[a]	0.393	0.375	0.396
My life would be better if I owned certain things I do not have	0.681	0.740	0.691
I wouldn't be happier if I owned nicer things[a]	0.287	0.534	0.199
I'd be happier if I could afford to buy more things	0.645	0.618	0.680
It sometimes bothers me quite a bit that I can't afford to buy all the things I'd like	0.524	0.473	0.468

[a]Indicate reversed items.

Table 7.   Latent means or subscales of material values.

	Success	Centrality	Happiness
Portugal	2.039	2.745	2.881
Spain	2.103	2.964	2.495
Germany	2.670	3.122	2.678

done by imposing a means factor of 0 on the reference country to determine the equality of the means for the other countries, or forcing equality of the means of each of the factors and for each country alternately.

Using Portugal as the country of reference, Tables 7 and 8 show the significant differences between the Portuguese sample and the other in terms of mean factors. Particularly, Table 8 shows the results of various mean

Table 8. Cross-national comparison of materialism scale means (base model: partial scalar invariance).

	Mean difference	Standardised error	Critical ratio	p
Compared to Portugal				
Spain				
Success	0.064	0.063	1.014	0.311
Centrality	0.219	0.076	2.892	0.004
Happiness	−0.385	0.047	8.113	0.000
Germany				
Success	0.631	0.074	8.496	0.000
Centrality	0.377	0.081	4.671	0.000
Happiness	−0.203	0.047	4.322	0.000
Compared to Spain				
Germany				
Success	0.567	0.083	6.837	0.000
Centrality	0.159	0.090	1.767	0.077
Happiness	0.183	0.050	3.669	0.000

comparison tests, where almost all means of the Portuguese sample are significantly different from the other samples. The German and the Portuguese sample have significant mean differences for all dimensions. The Spanish and the Portuguese sample have significantly different mean values for the Centrality and Happiness subscales ($p < 0.005$). These two countries present significantly higher means of materialism values related with Centrality in acquisition and Success. Portugal differs significantly with a higher Happiness dimension mean, confirming the pragmatism of Germans and Spanish (Hill, 2001) and their greater materialism when they are evaluating the success of people and the value they place on things. To the Portuguese, the need for goods is related to the ambition of achieving Happiness. However, there are no significant differences in the Success value of materialism between Portuguese and Spanish young people. With the restriction that the materialistic dimensions are zero to Spain, we find significant differences in Success and Happiness materialism values between the German and Spanish students (Table 7).

7. Materialism Values and Ambitions of Life

Following the methodology used by Richins and Dawson (1992), the distribution measures of each subscale were calculated. Supported by consistent reliability distributions for the overall materialism measure, three dimensions

Table 9.   Descriptive statistics for materialism scale and its components.

		Mean	SD	Range	Skew	Kurtosis
Portugal	Materialism	43.4675	6.93165	25–59	−0.146	−0.377
	Success	14.1195	3.60386	6–26	0.126	−0.138
	Centrality	16.5073	3.73807	7.29	0.224	−0.131
	Happiness	15.2788	3.22995	5–24	−0.338	−0.016
Spain	Materialism	42.1912	8.88808	20–80	0.553	0.865
	Success	14.5329	4.16386	6–30	0.501	0.432
	Centrality	17.1223	4.36403	6–30	0.321	0.295
	Happiness	13.0564	3.65018	5–25	0.118	0.231
Germany	Materialism	46.6782	8.01742	22–65	−0.474	0.194
	Success	16.9208	4.07073	6–27	0.117	−0.258
	Centrality	18.5941	3.84314	8–29	−0.072	−0.513
	Happiness	14.3960	3.49863	5–25	−0.087	−0.006

were determined to measure individual or cultural materialism characteristics. One approach is to use raw scores on each characteristic to establish scale reliabilities and standard norms; Table 9 presents this raw data for all measures and each subscale, along with the values for asymmetry and Kurtosis. These data were calculated by adding the raw scores on each item for each factor, according to Richins and Dawson's (1992) and Cousté and Orvaiz' (2001) methodology.

German students seem to be the only sample to show levels of materialism similar to the US samples, while Hispanic (Portuguese and Spanish) students present lower levels of materialism. The Success component seems similar between American students and the Latin young people, unlike German students who present higher levels of materialism. The Happiness component apparently is not different among American, German, and Spanish samples although the Portuguese sample shows higher levels of materialism to achieve happiness. Otherwise Centrality in acquisition seems to be a stronger materialism value in American young adults.

Based on a question about 14 ambitions and life objectives, respondents were asked to classify them on a 5-point Likert scale (5 extremely important; 1 not important). A comparison of ambitions between individuals who score higher in materialism with those who score lower in materialism of each country, and with the original sample, did not confirm the idea that materialistic people are more likely to value their comfort and possessions than friendship and family.

Respondents were divided into terciles, according to the methodology used in the original study, based on their materialism scores. The percentage of respondents, including each value in their three choices, was examined.

Table 9 presents the mean scored for each subscale by different groups of individuals. The first tercil represents respondents higher in materialism (materialism mean value scale $= 51.43$ for Portugal; 52.63 for Spain; 55.58 for Germany) and the third tercil are those with a lower score in materialism (materialism mean value scale $= 35.09$ for Portugal; 32.78 for Spain; 37.4 for Germany). Using the descriptive statistics for materialism scales, the percentages of young adults that rate each of the objectives as very or extremely important (4 and 5) were compared (Table 10).

The findings show that approximately 80–99% of materialistic youth consider their ambitions — "Be successful in your chosen career", "Be happy", "Have a comfortable life", "True friendship", and "Self-respect" — to be "very" or "extremely important". Only 31% of respondents indicated the highest score for "Develop your sporting talents".

Overall, the most valued ambitions are very similar for young adults in European countries. However, some differences are apparent on several items in these three countries: "Get married and have a family", "Start your own business", and "Have social recognition". Having a family appears to be important to all Portuguese young adults although not for Spanish young adults; the same item only matters to the higher materialistic German young adults. "Start your own business" is also classified as very important in the Portuguese sample but not in the others. "Have social recognition" is important to all higher materialistic young adults, although valued differently, with less than 23% of Portuguese, 44% of Spanish, and 63% of German young adults.

As expected, respondents higher in materialism are more likely to value "Be successful in your chosen career", "Make a lot of money", and "Have social recognition", but less likely to value "Inner harmony". These are the significantly common differences between higher and lower score materialism young adults in the three countries.

The *caliente* culture, designated by Hill (2001) to classify the Spanish culture, seems to explain the ambitions or objectives more likely to be valued by the Spanish youth. Those who are lower in materialism are more likely to value "Take care of loving ones" and "True friendship".

The individualistic and pragmatic (Hofstede, 1997) characteristics of German and Spanish cultures, for those revealing higher levels of materialism, are revealed by the differentiated life-ambition item, "Have a comfortable life".

The converging process among European countries, not only at an economic and infra-structure level (Ganesh, 1998), but also in terms of cultural, social, and consumer values (Boutonnat *et al.*, 1991), still maintains

Table 10. Percent of respondents high and low in materialism that indicate aspirations in life as very or extremely important.

Aspirações na vida	Portugal					Spain					Germany				
	HM %		LM %		Dif.	HM %		LM %		Dif.	HM %		LM %		Dif.
Get married and have a family	55.1	145	56.9	137	-1.8	36.4	96	36.6	101	-0.2	43.4	53	27.9	61	15.5
Travel the world	54.5	145	47.4	137	7.1	40.6	96	47.5	101	-6.9	52.8	53	49.2	63	3.6
Start your own business	49.0	145	48.6	136	0.4	33.3	96	25.0	100	8.3	37.8	53	25.8	62	12.0
Be successful in your chosen career	93.8	145	86.0	136	7.8*	85.8	96	70.3	101	15.5*	83.0	53	58.7	63	24.3*
Make a lot of money	67.6	145	37.5	136	30.1*	64.6	96	24.0	100	40.6*	64.1	53	15.9	63	48.2*
Be happy	98.6	145	98.5	137	0.1	95.8	96	98.0	101	-2.2	92.5	53	95.3	64	-2.8
Develop your sporting talents	26.2	145	30.2	136	-4.0	18.7	96	21.3	99	-2.6	17.0	53	20.6	63	-3.6
Be totally independent	74.4	144	77.4	137	-3.0	60.5	96	69.0	100	-8.5	43.4	53	27.0	63	16.4
Have a comfortable life	89.7	145	83.2	137	6.5	84.3	96	68.3	101	14.0*	84.9	53	40.7	64	44.2*
Have social recognition	22.8	145	13.1	137	9.7*	43.7	96	15.0	100	28.7*	62.2	53	33.8	62	28.4*
True friendship	93.8	145	97.1	137	-3.3	89.6	96	97.0	100	-7.4*	92.4	53	95.1	62	-2.7
Take care of loved ones	79.9	144	88.3	137	-8.4	81.3	96	98.0	100	-12.7*	71.7	53	82.2	62	-10.5
Self respect	93.8	145	97.1	137	-3.3	89.6	96	92.0	100	-2.4	80.7	52	76.2	63	4.5
Inner harmony	86.9	145	94.9	137	-8.0*	71.9	96	88.1	101	-16.2*	67.9	53	95.2	62	-27.3*

Note: HM: higher in materialism; LM: lower in materialism; *p < 0.05.

differences and divergences (Polonsky *et al.*, 2001). This study confirms the divergences of interest and appeal that could differentiate the European young adult consumers. They share objectives and ambitions, but reflect different values in the way they face life and consumption. The way to influence these different young adults is through different images and environments that transmit happiness to the Portuguese, success to Germans, and possession to the Spanish.

8. Conclusions, Limitations and Implications

The findings based on multiple-group analysis show evidence of measurement equivalence among cultures. The results correspond closely to those reported by Richins and Dawson (1992) and respect the testing procedure proposed by Steenkamp and Baumgartner (1998). The scale, therefore, appears to be useful in other Western cultures. Support for partial metric invariance and partial scalar invariance also exists, implying that ratings on the materialism scale can be cross-nationally compared. The factor variances are only partially invariant, implying that the young people of different countries present significant differences in the way they evaluate success. However, the composite reliability estimates support internal consistency of the materialism scales.

Differences in materialism among young Europeans are evident in their consideration of the various dimensions and the way each is analysed. This inevitably results in differences in attitudes, concept interpretation, and expectations. Further difference can be expected in kindness and understanding of advertising. The highest evaluation of the Happiness factor by young Portuguese suggests that images and ideas associating happiness with possession will be more readily embraced, through both challenges (like taste tests) or particular ads. Faced with ads or brand images that relate possession to success or the pleasure of future acquisition, young Germans and Spanish will respond more readily, although the latter value possession to best enjoy life.

The mean comparison tests show significant mean differences on the materialism measure for success, as expected, and for the centrality and happiness scales. Different scores of means are presented connected with the different cultures. Portugal presents more sentimental values with higher levels linking materialism to happiness. The higher level of wealth in Spain and Germany is reflected in the superior levels of materialism associated with objectives of possession and acquisition. This study also supports the conclusion of other researchers that materialistic people value material possessions more than those that report low levels of materialism.

While the dimensions and item loadings are similar in this study, the analysis of the results and comparison with American young people indicated several differences of materialism levels among Americans, Portuguese, Germans, and Spanish. While differences of item loadings have also been found, there are several reasons for these differences: (1) the underlying meanings of some questions may be interpreted differently by consumers in different countries; (2) cultural norms of deference and politeness may originate answering differences; (3) different stages of economic development imply different levels of consumer purchasing power in these countries and these differences are reflected in attitudes and materialism of individuals; (4) the markets in these different countries display differences in maturity and disposable commodities.

This study has several limitations. First, a modified conceptual model is used, which can limit comparisons with the American sample. Second, several methodological issues used, related to international comparison, can influence results and weaken the findings. The findings would be much more powerful in data collected randomly among young adult consumers in various countries.

To improve international comparison research, items must be created that can be used in different countries or cultures without misperception or misinterpretation. It is also extremely important to have similar samples from different countries. The present samples were obtained directly in universities, which is not the case for the American sample. The average age of students in Germany is also a bit higher than in Portugal and Spain. The demographic and psychological characteristics of the different samples could be different, and such differences could influence the validity of the findings.

The third improvement relates to the validity of the instrument in different languages in international comparison studies. The same sentence in different languages could have different subtleties in meaning and possible translation errors could further aggravate the actual differences when the instrument is administered in different cultures. More careful translation procedures, such as "decentred" translation or nonliteral translation (Werner and Campbell, 1970) or "back translation" (Triandis, 1972), should be adapted in future research to ensure the validity of the instrument used in different languages.

Another limitation of this study is related to the scale used. Richins (2004) propose another short form of materialism scale because the problems verified in cross-cultural studies based on the original scale (Richins and Dawson, 1992). The reverse-coded items can cause failure of fit scales (Wong *et al.*, 2003) and social norms of each culture could predispose the answers to assume certain answering tendency (Mick, 1996). Those identified evidence could demolish our conclusions.

The findings of this study have implications for consumer education. The study confirmed the three dimensions of consumer materialism values and the results can be used to develop better consumer materialism values guidelines in consumer behaviour. The similarities and differences between the European and American consumers found in this study can be used to help students and business better understand different attitudes and consumer behaviour from different cultures. This study can serve as a reference to provide background information and to understand consumer behaviour toward advertising, image, and brands in Europe.

References

Abela, A (2006). Marketing and consumerism: A response to O'Shaughnessy and O'Shaughnessy. *European Journal of Marketing* 40(1/2), 5–16.

Alsop, R (19 January 1988). Mom leaves her mark in loyalty to products. *The Wall Street Journal*, 33.

Arbuckle, J and W Wothke (1999). *AMOS 4.0 User's Guide*. Chicago: SmallWaters Corporation.

Bachman, G (1997). Materialism values and susceptibility to influence in children. *Advances in Consumer Research*, 24, 82–88.

Belk, R (1985). Materialism: Trait aspects of living in the material world. *Journal of Consumer Research*, 12(3), 265–280.

Boutonnat, Y, A Bauer and M Ottenfeld (1991). North American and European markets...Is each homogeneous or heterogeneous? *Applied Marketing Research*, 31(1), 9–16.

Brée, J (1993). *Les Enfants, La Consommation et le Marketing* [Children, Consumption and Marketing]. Paris: Presses Universitaires de France.

Bronwne, B and D Kaldenberg (1997). Conceptualising self-monitoring: Links to materialism and product involvement. *Journal of Consumer Marketing*, 14(1), 31–44.

Byrne, B (2001). *Structural Equation Modeling with AMOS: Basics Concepts, Applications, and Programming*. New Jersey: Lawrence Erlbaum Associates.

Byrne, B (1998). *Structural Equation Modeling with LISREL, PRELIS, and SIMPLIS: Basics Concepts, Applications, and Programming*. New Jersey: Lawrence Erlbaum Associates.

Campbell, C (1987). *The Romantic Ethic and the Spirit of Modern Consumerism*. New York: Basil Blackwell.

Carlson, L, S Grossbart and A Walsh (1990). Mother's communication orientation and consumer-socialisation tendencies. *Journal of Advertising*, 19(3), 27–38.

Chan, K (2006a). Exploring children's perceptions of material posessions: A drawing study. *Qualitative Market Research*, 9(4), 352–370.

Chan, K (2006b). Materialism among adolescents in urban China. *Young Consumers*, 7(2), 64–75.

Chang, L and R Arkin (2002). Materialism as an attempt to cope with uncertainty. *Psychology & Marketing*, 19(5), 389–406.

Christopher, AN, RD Morgan, P Marek, M Keller and K Drummand (2005). Materialism and self-presentational styles. *Personality and Individual Differences*, 38, 137–149.

Clark, P, C Martin and A Bush (2001). The effect of role model influence on Adolescents' Materialism and Marketplace Knowledge. *Journal of Marketing Theory and Practice*, 9(4), 27–36.

Cousté, N and M Orvaiz (2000). Materialismo y Comportamiento del Consumidor: Un Estudio Exploratorio de los Jóvenes [Materialism and Consumer Behaviour: Exploratory Study of Young People]. Unpublished Paper.

Dittmar, H and L Pepper (1994). To have is to be: Materialism and person perception in working-class and middle-class British adolescents. *Journal of Economic Psychology*, 15, 233–251.

Douglas, S and S Craig (1983). *International Marketing Research*. New Jersey: Prentice-Hall.

Durvasula, S, S Lysonski and JC Andrews (1993). Cross-cultural generalizability of a scale for profiling consumers' decision-making styles. *The Journal of Consumer Affairs*, 27(1), 55–65.

Durvasula, S, S Lysonski and J Watson (2001). Does vanity describe other cultures? A cross-cultural examination of the vanity scale. *The Journal of Consumer Affairs*, 35(1), 180–199.

Eastman, JK, B Fredenberger, D Campbell and S Calvert (1997). The relationship between status consumption and materialism: A cross-cultural comparison of Chinese, Mexican and American Students. *Journal of Marketing Theory and Practice*, 5(1), 52–66.

Englis, B and M Solomon (1995). To be and not to be: Lifestyle imagery, reference groups, and the clustering of America. *Journal of Advertising*, 24(1), 13–25.

Englis, B, M Solomon and A Olofsson (1993). Consumption imagery in music television: A bi-cultural perspective. *Journal of Advertising*, 22(4), 21–33.

Fournier, S and M Richins (1991). Some theoretical and popular notions concerning materialism. *Journal of Social Behaviour and Personality*, 6, 403–414.

Ganesh, J (1998). Converging trends within the European Union: Insights from an analysis of diffusion patterns. *Journal of International Marketing*, 6(4), 32–48.

Ger, G and R Belk (1996). Cross-cultural differences in materialism. *Journal of Economic Psychology*, 17, 55–77.

Gerbner, G, L Gross, N Signorielli and M Morgan (1980). Aging with television: Images on television drama and conceptions of social reality. *Journal of Communication*, 30(1), 37–47.

Graham, L and L Hamdan (1987). *Youthtrends — capturing the $200 Billion Youth Market*. New York: St Martin's Press.

Hair, J, RL Tatham, RE Anderson and W Black (1998). *Multivariate Data Analysis*, 5th Ed. New Jersey: Prentice-Hall.

Hill, R (2001). *Nós Europeus* [We Europeans]. Porto: Edições Asa.

Hofstede, G (1997). *Culture's Consequences: International Differences in Work-Related Values*. Beverly Hills: Sage Publications.

Kamakura, W and T Novak (1992). Value-system segmentation: Exploring the meaning of LOV. *Journal of Consumer Research*, 19(1), 119–132.

Kilbourne, W, M Grunhagen and J Foley (2005). A cross-cultural examination of the relationship between materialism and individual values. *Journal of Economic Psychology*, 26(5), 624–635.

Lastovicka, J (1982). On the validation of lifestyle traits: A review and illustration. *Journal of Marketing Research*, 29(1), 126–138.

Leung, K and M Bond (1989). On the empirical identification of dimensions for cross-cultural comparisons. *Journal of Cross-Cultural Psychology*, 20(2), 133–151.

Li, F, P Harmer and A Acock (1996). The task and ego orientations in sport questionnaire: Construct equivalence and mean differences across gender. *Research Quartely for Exercise and Sport*, 68(2), 228–238.

Marsh, H, I Marco and H Apçý (2002). Cross-cultural validity of the physical self-description questionnaire: Comparison of factor structures in Australia, Spain, and Turkey. *Research Quartely for Exercise and Sport*, 73(3), 257–270.

Mick, D (1996). Are studies of dark side variables confounded by socially desirable responding? The case of materialism. *Journal of Consumer Research*, 23(2), 106–119.

Mukerji, C (1983). *From Graven Images: Patterns of Modern Materialism*. New York: Columbia University Press.

Muncy, J and J Eastman (1998). Materialism and consumer ethics: An exploratory study. *Journal of Business Ethics*, 17(2), 137–145.

Myers, M *et al.* (2000). Academic insights: An application of multiple-group causal models in assessing cross-cultural measurement equivalence. *Journal of International Marketing*, 8(4), 108–121.

O'Guinn, T and R Faber (1989). Compulsive buying: A phenomenological exploration. *Journal of Consumer Research*, 16, 147–157.

O'Guinn, T and L Shrum (1997). The role of television in the construction of consumer reality. *Journal of Consumer Research*, 23(4), 278–294.

Otnes, C and L Scott (1996). Something old, something new: Exploring the interaction between ritual and advertising. *Journal of Advertising*, 25(1), 33–50.

Polonsky, MJ, PQ Brito, J Pinto and N Higgs-Kleyn (2001). Consumer ethics in European Union: A comparison of northern and southern views. *Journal of Business Ethics*, 31(2), 117–130.

Rassuli, K and S Hollander (1986). Desire — Induce, innate, insatiable? *Journal of Macromarketing*, 6(2), 4–24.

Richins, M (2004). The material values: Measurement properties and development of a short form. *Journal of Consumer Research*, 31(1), 209–219.

Richins, M (1994). Special possessions and the expression of material values. *Journal of Consumer Research*, 21(3), 522–533.

Richins, M and S Dawson (1992). A consumer values orientation for materialism and its measurement: Scale development and validation. *Journal of Consumer Research*, 19(3), 312–325.

Rindfleisch, A, J Burroughs and F Denton (1997). Family structure, materialism, and compulsive consumption. *Journal of Consumer Research*, 23(4), 312–325.

Roberts, J (1998). Compulsive buying among college students: An investigation of its antecedents, consequences, and implications for public policy. *The Journal of Consumer Affairs*, 32(2), 295–319.

Roberts, J, C Manolis and J Tanner (2006). Adolescent autonomy and the impact of family structure on materialism and compulsive buying. *Journal of Marketing Theory and Practice*, 14(4), 301–314.

Roberts, J, C Manolis and J Tanner (2003). Family structure, materialism, and compulsive buying: A reinquiry and extension. *Academy of Marketing Science Journal*, 31(3), 300–318.

Rose, G (1999). Consumer socialisation, parental style, and developmental timetables in the United States and Japan. *Journal of Marketing*, 63(3), 105–119.

Salgueiro, M and E Reis (2000). Socialização dos Jovens no Trabalho: Aplicação de um Modelo de Equações Estruturais. In *Métodos Quantitativos*, 1st Ed. Elizabeth Reis e Manuel Ferreira, Edições Sílabo, Lisboa.

Sproles, E and G Sproles (1990). Consumer decision-making styles as a function of individual learning styles. *The Journal of Consumer Affairs*, 24(1), 134–147.

Steenkamp, J-B and H Baumgartner (1998). Assessing measurement invariance in cross-national consumer research. *Journal of Consumer Research*, 25(1), 78–90.

Triandis, H (1972). *The Analysis of Subjective Culture*. New York: Wiley.

Twitchell, J (2000). In defense of materialism. *Across the Board*, 37(3), 64–69.

Wallendorf, M and E Arnould (1988). "My favorite things": A cross-cultural inquiry into objects attachment, possessiveness, and social linkage. *Journal of Consumer Research*, 14(4), 531–547.

Walsh, G, V Mitchell and T Thurau (2001). German consumer decision-making styles. *The Journal of Consumer Affairs*, 35(1), 73–95.

Wang, J and M Wallendorf (2006). Materialism, status signaling, and product satifaction. *Academy of Marketing Science Journal*, 34(4), 494–505.

Ward, S and D Wackman (1971). Family and media influences on adolescent consumer learning. *American Behavioural Scientist*, 14, 415–427.

Webster, C and R Beatty (1997). Nationality, materialism, and possession importance. *Advances in Consumer Research*, 24, 204–208.

Werner, O and D Campbell (1970). Translating, working through Interpreters, and the Problem of Decentring. In *Handbook of Method in Cultural Anthropology*, R Naroll and R Cohen (eds.) pp. 398–420. American Museum of Natural History.

Wong, N, A Rindfleisch and J Burroughs (2003). Do reverse-worded items confound measures in cross-cultural consumer research? The case of the material values scale. *Journal of Consumer Research*, 30(1), 72–91.

Zhang, Y and B Gelb (1996). Matching advertising appeals to culture: The influence of products' use conditions. *Journal of Advertising*, 25(3), 29–46.

7

IMPLEMENTING SERVICES IN PRICING DECISIONS TO ENHANCE THE CUSTOMER RELATIONSHIP — A FRAMEWORK FOR PRICE SETTING

Sören Lüders* and Luisa Andreu

University of Valencia, Spain

Anna S. Mattila

Pennsylvania State University, USA

This study develops a pricing framework that focuses on relationship-building — a factor that has been largely ignored in the pricing literature. First, a case-study method has been employed to better understand how a production-oriented company sets prices for its products. Then a framework has been developed which incorporates the service component in the pricing equation. The results of this research suggest that factoring in the price for services offered can enhance relationship management, thus having a positive impact on the company's business performance.

Keywords: Pricing; services; customer relationship management; case study.

1. Introduction

Globalisation has intensified competition across product categories, thus making it increasingly difficult for companies to grow and to remain

---

*Corresponding author.

profitable. The marketing mix, including pricing, is one of the key elements in helping companies to face this new challenge. For example, an improvement of 1% in price yields higher gains in operating profits than similar improvements in variable costs, fixed costs, or volume (Eugster *et al.*, 2000). Despite the strong link between pricing and bottom-line, pricing remains one of the least researched areas in marketing (Hoffmann *et al.*, 2002). One potential reason for ignorance in the pricing arena is the scarcity of managerial tools in the complex process of price-setting (McCarthy and Perrault, 1993). Today's dynamic business environment clearly calls for a more systematic approach to pricing (Samiee, 1987).

In the course of the past years the view of pricing as a strategic element has changed. Traditionally, the price of a unit or a service was defined as the number of monetary units the customer is willing to pay to receive the goods (Simon, 1989; Kotler *et al.*, 1999). More recent conceptualisations view pricing from the customer's perspective, i.e., what is given up or sacrificed to obtain the good (Zeithaml *et al.*, 1988; Thompson and Coe, 1997). Yet, only few firms exploit the opportunity of customer-based pricing strategies (Sotgui and Ancarani, 2004). By taking the customers' point of view into account, companies can strengthen customer relationships, which in turn results in lower price elasticity, lower fluctuation in the customer base, and higher profits (Reichheld and Sasser, 1998). For the incorporation of the customer perspective into pricing decisions, more complex pricing tools or methods are needed (Gijsbrechts and Campo, 2000).

The goal of this study is to develop a managerially oriented pricing framework. A case-study method is used to illustrate how a traditional manufacturing firm sets its prices and how the company's service offerings can be employed to enhance relationship-building. More specifically, our research objectives are as follows:

1. To identify the key factors influencing a company's price-setting practices.
2. To analyse the importance of customer orientation for pricing decisions and the role of services in this process.
3. To provide managerial guidelines for pricing decisions.

The structure of this chapter is as follows: First, we present a conceptual background on pricing and research questions. Second, we explain the research methodology and our results. The final section of the chapter describes our customer-oriented pricing framework.

2. Theoretical Background and Research Questions

2.1. *Factors influencing price setting*

Factors influencing pricing can be separated into two types: internal and external. External elements include the company's access to critical resources, market-related economic factors, and industry-related economic factors, while internal elements represent restrictions within the company (Lancioni *et al.*, 2005). A clear understanding of these factors is a prerequisite for effective price-setting (Forman and Hunt 2004; Hinterhuber 2004; Myers, Cavusgil and Diamatopoulus, 2002; Marsh, 2000).

The goal of this study is to develop a clear and structured guideline for managerial price-setting practices. To that end, we will first identify the most salient factors in driving managers' pricing decisions, thus leading to the following research question (RQ):

RQ1: What are the most important factors and objectives influencing managers' price-setting practices?

2.2. *Building of customer relationships and pricing*

Price, as any element of the marketing mix, should focus on building customer loyalty via relationships management (Sawhney and Kotler, 2001). Company reputation, which is closely related to relationship-building, can have a significant effect on the customer's perception of the company's pricing structure and offer (Cox, 2001). It is crucial to gain an understanding of how different consumers value the company's products and service offerings. Observing the consumer and their purchasing decisions enables the company to react quickly to changes and to better satisfy customers' needs (Qu and Ennew, 2003). Due to price elasticity or different key elements in the purchase decision process, customers are willing to pay varying prices for the same product. Incorporating these differences into price structures would add value to the customer and the company alike, which should be a main purpose of marketing strategies (Anderson and Narus, 1999). In addition to this, satisfying customers' needs and creating value will give the company a competitive advantage (Kothandaraman and Wilson, 2001). Surprisingly, only few companies base their pricing decisions on customer relationships and their purchasing behavior (Sotgui and Ancarani, 2004). To bridge that gap, we address the following research question:

RQ2: How important is customer orientation in the price-setting process and what role do services offers play in pricing?

2.3. Coordinating activities

One of the main obstacles in the context of pricing is that decisions are made locally without any centralised efforts (Smith, 1995). The lack of clear pricing strategies leads to ill-defined single-step decisions. The upper management might have a long-term view and focus on profit margins, while the sales force follows a short-term approach and tends to focus on local competition (Myers, 1997). This narrow focus might lead to inefficiencies and lost profits. Effective communication and a shared vision are the cornerstones of successful implementation of company strategies, including pricing objectives or service offerings (Shimp, 2003). It is not only important to identify the main variables influencing the price, but also the coordinating activities in the overall price-setting process and its main elements. This leads us to the following research question:

RQ3: To what extend are pricing process and the element of the service offered coordinated?

An overall structure of our conceptual framework is shown in Figure 1.

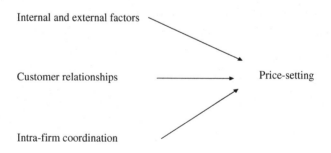

Figure 1.   Framework structure.

3. Research Methodology

A case-study method was chosen to explore our objectives, because of the complex nature of pricing processes. Especially if multifaceted processes are being studied and input of real-world data is used to form concepts, qualitative methods such as case studies are appropriate (Yin, 1994; Gummesson, 2004).

A company[1] operating globally was selected for our purpose. The strategic situation of the case organisation, defined by a highly competitive and international market, made this scenario very attractive for our study. The customer-relationship management and maintenance as well as an effective pricing strategy are essential in such an environment.

In-depth interviews revealed that pricing decisions in this company are made by specific, higher rank managers. Consequently, data collection was limited to ten pricing experts. Respondents were prescreened for their leadership position and for their active participation in the company's pricing policies.

A structured e-mail survey was sent out in two stages. The first phase of the data collection gathered general information, including an overview of various decision-making processes across different management levels (e.g., Department and Business Development Managers vs. Unit Sales Managers, Directing Managers, Assistant, and Vice President). The second round of the e-mail interviews focused on price-setting.

Prior literature on pricing combined with our initial in-depth interviews was used as input into the survey development. The questionnaire included a list of potential factors influencing managers' pricing decisions (Marsh, 2000; Myers *et al.*, 2002; Forman and Hunt, 2004; Lancioni, 2005). The ten expert managers were asked to specify the significance of these factors using a semantic differential scale. In addition, a 5-point Likert scale was used to capture the guidelines in the pricing process (Myers *et al.*, 2002; Forman and Hunt, 2004; Avlonitis and Indounas, 2005).

---

[1]The company — Holley — is a conglomerate with 11 branches and 7 main business areas such as: Metrological Instruments, Power Automation, Information Technology, Biopharmaceuticals, Chemical, Real Estate, and Special Micro Motors. Offices and production facilities are located in Asia, USA, South America, Europe, and Africa. Therefore, its business spreads over different geographical areas and several markets. The company is the market leader in China for electricity meters, and is pursuing a global leadership for electric products and utility meters. Another main product is the first herbal medicine against malaria conforming to Western medicine standards that has been ratified by the World Health Organisation (WHO).

4. Results

Table 1 shows the consensus of the experts' opinions reflecting pricing principles. The main findings are that numerous factors influence the pricing
process and that, although several important objectives for price-setting were
identified in our research, one main objective is followed in the long run. Furthermore, it was identified that the pricing strategy is changed according to
different customer groups and that service offerings are an important element
to enhance the customer relationship.

4.1. *Salient factors and pricing objectives*

The participants were asked to assess several internal and external factors
that influence their pricing decisions. Internal factors include the company's
overall marketing strategy, production costs (salaries, rent, etc.), costs of raw
materials, and costs of service offerings. External factors reflect competitive
forces, market price of the offered products, position in the market, and the
volume of the orders. Table 2 shows internal and external elements that influence the managers' pricing decisions. The results are congruent with prior
research indicating that pricing decisions are affected by several factors (Lancioni, 2005). As shown in Table 2, the majority of participants ranked factors
such as competitive actions and cost of raw materials as most influential elements. This is not surprising, given the heavy emphasis on cost structures,
especially in a manufacturing setting. More importantly, the service component was rated as a highly influential factor in the pricing process.

The state of the local economy does not seem to play an important role in
the price-setting process. The consensus in Table 1 shows that a majority of
the interviewees agreed with this point put forward. When asked about this
factor, 28.6% disagreed, 28.6% neither agreed nor disagreed, and 42.9%
of the respondents tended to agree (28.6%) or strongly agree (14.3%) with
evaluating the factor as not important for the price-setting. These findings are
congruent with previous research in pricing. If markets are becoming more
homogenous the differences between countries are not as important anymore
(Samiee and Roth, 1992; Yip, 1989). Therefore we will not consider this
factor as one of the most influential factors for our price-setting framework.

Pricing objectives are the basis for the price-setting process (Oxenfeldt,
1983). For that reason we asked the participants to identify their main pricing objectives. Our findings shown in Table 3 are compatible with the notion
that companies typically follow several pricing objectives (Avlonitis and

Table 1. Consensus of opinions and summary of the main guiding pricing principles.

	Strongly disagree		Disagree		Neither agree nor disagree		Agree		Strongly agree		Median
	Frequency	%	Frequency	%	Frequency	%	Frequency	%	Frequency	%	
Statement 1: A lot of factors influence pricing, but the economy of a country does not influence the decision very much											
	—	—	2	28.6	2	28.6	2	28.6	1	14.3	3.29
Statement 2: The company has one main pricing objective (long-term growth)											
	—	—	—	—	4	57.1	3	42.9	—	—	3.43
Statement 3: The pricing strategy is not changed for different situations or customer groups											
	3	42.9	2	28.6	1	14.3	1	14.3	—	—	2.00
Statement 4: Overall, there is one main pricing strategy in the long run											
	—	—	1	14.3	1	14.3	5	71.4	—	—	3.57
Statement 5: Services can be used to enhance the relationship to the customer											
	—	—	—	—	—	—	2	28.6	5	71.4	4.71

Table 2. Factors influencing the price.

Factors	Not at all important		Not so important		Hard to decide		Fairly important		Very important	
	Frequency	%	Frequency	%	Frequency	%	Frequency	%	Frequency	%
Competitors	1	10	—	—	—	—	—	—	9	90
Raw materials	1	10	—	—	—	—	3	30	6	60
Production costs	1	10	—	—	2	20	4	40	3	30
Market price	1	10	1	10	—	—	4	40	4	40
Strategy	1	10	—	—	1	10	5	50	3	30
Position	1	10	2	20	1	10	5	50	1	10
Service	—	—	1	10	2	20	5	50	2	20
Volume	1	10	—	—	1	10	7	70	1	10

Note: $n = 10$; (1) not at all important to (5) very important.

Table 3.   Pricing objectives.

Objectives	Strongly disagree		Disagree		Neither agree nor disagree		Agree		Strongly agree	
	Frequency	%	Frequency	%	Frequency	%	Frequency	%	Frequency	%
Price maximisation	1	10	—	—	2	20	5	50	2	20
Sales maximisation	—	—	2	20	—	—	5	50	3	30
Market share	—	—	1	10	2	20	3	30	4	40
Cover costs	—	—	—	—	3	30	7	70	—	—
Relation to customer	—	—	—	—	2	20	5	50	3	30
Price stability	—	—	—	—	3	30	7	70	—	—
Long-term growth	—	—	—	—	3	30	1	10	6	60

Note: $n = 10$; (1) strongly disagree to (5) strongly agree.

Indounas, 2005; Diamantopoulus 1991). The findings also demonstrate that customer relations are considered to be one of the more important objectives.

4.2. Customer orientation and the role of services

Table 1 shows that the pricing strategies are adapted to various customer groups or strategic situations. Also the respondents were surveyed regarding their views on how to improve the customer relationship (Table 4) and on attributes of importance from the customer's perspective (Table 5). It is interesting to note that services were considered a way to improve customer relationships by most participants and that these relationships are highly salient in the customer's mind. Similar results were obtained for product quality. Price, on the other hand, was considered a critical attribute in its own right, but not having a major impact on relationship-building and maintenance.

All respondents agreed with the last statement in Table 1 that services can be used to enhance customer relationships. This study therefore provides further evidence for the usefulness of services in enhancing customer relations. This even applies to companies that so far have not emphasised their service offerings and have not implemented them in their pricing strategy.

4.3. Intra-firm coordination

Although the service component is surfaced as a key element of the pricing process, it is not clear how such services should be delivered (please refer to Table 6). Two-thirds of the respondents declared the department manager responsible for services offered, and yet other stakeholders were also identified. This relatively scattered approach can lead to a rather unstructured process and lack of coordination of service activities.

Services have been identified as an important element in pricing and a lack of coordination can have similar effects on the performance of the company as uncoordinated price-setting can have. The needs of the customer might not be addressed correctly, which would lead to dissatisfaction, increase in fluctuation, and decreasing profits.

5.   A Pricing Framework

Pricing is a complex and multifaceted phenomenon (Diamantopoulus and Mathews, 1995). In this study, we combine customer-based and cost-based

Table 4. Ways to improve customer relationships.

Ways to improve customer relationship	Strongly disagree		Disagree		Neither agree nor disagree		Agree		Strongly agree	
	Frequency	%	Frequency	%	Frequency	%	Frequency	%	Frequency	%
Visits	—	—	—	—	1	10	5	50	4	40
Services	—	—	—	—	2	20	5	50	3	30
Quality	—	—	—	—	1	10	4	40	5	50
Promotions	1	10	—	—	3	30	5	50	1	10
Fairs	1	10	—	—	2	20	6	60	1	10

Note: $n = 10$; (1) strongly disagree to (5) strongly agree.

Table 5.   Key elements from customer's perspectives.

Factors	Not at all important		Not so important		Hard to decide		Fairly important		Very important	
	Frequency	%	Frequency	%	Frequency	%	Frequency	%	Frequency	%
Price	1	10	1	10	1	10	5	50	2	20
Quality	—	—	1	10	1	10	4	40	4	40
Relationship	—	—	1	11.1	1	11.1	6	66.7	1	11.1

Note: $n = 10$; (1) not at all important/strongly disagree (5) very important/strongly agree.

Table 6. Responsibility for service offerings.

	Sales agent (%)	Other company (%)	Service department (%)	Department manager (%)	Senior management (%)
Yes	0	33.3	44.4	66.7	33.3
No	60	66.7	55.6	33.3	66.7

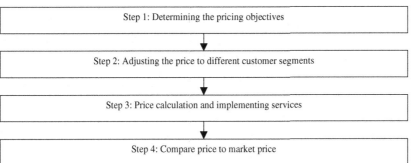

Figure 2. Structure for the development of the pricing framework.

approaches in a comprehensive framework that includes services as a key pricing component. Figure 2 provides a step-by-step overview of our pricing model.

The first step is to determine the company's pricing objectives. This is followed by a careful examination of the company's target markets. In the third step, a customer-centred pricing approach is developed. The pricing calculations are based on a modified cost-oriented approach. The customer perspective is reflected in the premium in respect of the value-added for a particular customer or customer group. The last step involves comparing the calculated price with average competitive market prices.

5.1. First step: Determining the pricing objectives

The company's pricing objectives act as guidelines throughout the process. Typically, companies have several pricing objectives, and hence they all need to be incorporated into the price-setting process (Oxenfeldt, 1983; Diamantopoulus, 1991). Our results are congruent with this multifaceted view. In this study, eight pricing objectives and eight internal and external factors were identified as important elements of the pricing process. Yet, determining the causal relationship between pricing objectives and factors affecting the final price can be tricky. In a study conducted by Avlonitis and Indounas (2005) the objective of maximising profits was important for markets with high competition, well-informed customers, and for companies with a competitive advantage. Additional objectives (important regardless of the market structure) were long-term growth and cost coverage. Our discussions with expert-managers identified highly similar objectives.

5.2.   Second step: Adjusting the price to different customer segments

Our results show that pricing strategies are adjusted according to different customer groups. Segmentation is crucial in order to understand if different customer groups are willing to pay a differential price for the company's products and services (Forsyth *et al.*, 2000).

Customers can be segmented into groups based on company size, purchase order volume, geographical area, or purchase reason. Customers' purchase reasons are influenced by factors such as quality, price, or certain service offerings. To address customer needs more effectively, the key elements in their purchase decision-making process have to be identified. In the present study, customer relationships has been identified as a salient factor in addition to product quality and price. Furthermore, the study results indicate that service offerings can enhance relationship building. These critical elements need to be entered into the price equation.

5.3.   Third step: Price calculation and implementing services

The price calculation in this chapter is based on the synthetic multi-step pricing approach presented by Tung *et al.*, (1997). More specifically, Hoffmann and Arnold's (1989) cost-oriented method has been slightly modified.

The present pricing model includes traditional cost-oriented factors such as fixed costs, variable costs, and a profit goal plus factors that make up the extended model. The first step is to calculate a basis for the price by using the traditional cost-oriented approach. For this the fixed costs (Fc), variable costs (Vc), and a margin or profit goal (Pg) of the company are combined. The fixed costs are adjusted by a certain percentage (PC), depending on how much of the total capacity or of the total of the fixed costs is used for a product. In the next step a service premium (Sp) is added to represent the added value for the customer by the service offerings. In the present approach an adjusted activity-based costing (ABC) approach has been used to calculate the premium. While traditional cost systems work well for homogeneous products, their underlying assumptions do not hold with services.

The ABC method first identifies activities being performed and then determines their associated costs. The activities can be roughly divided into two main categories. Unit-level activities (Ua) are performed for every unit of service produced and batch-level activities (Ba) for each set up of work. Other activities (Oa) enable the company to provide the service to the customer. The use of the ABC method for the service premium also helps to determine the customer's profitability. The method can pinpoint the differences in the costs of serving different customers. A customer who orders a large quantity might not be as profitable as one with a lower order volume. The reason for this lies in the specifications of the order or the different activities that have to be performed to fulfil the need of the customer. The traditional cost system considers changes in volume to reduce costs and not activities or services like the ABC approach, because it assumes that the overall usage of the company's resources is typical of resource usage for each product. If the resource requirements for an order vary from the typical of total expected company resources due to changes in activities, the ABC approach reflects the changes in costs and price more accurately (Lere, 2000). Therefore, if a constant market price has been taken as a basis, an order of large quantity with a variety of specifications can severely increase the costs and be less profitable than a much smaller order with less or no extra activities to be performed.

All elements together build the price for the product, including the basic costs and added value. The calculation of the price can be written as follows:

$$\text{Base} : (Fc * PC) + Vc + Pg$$
$$\text{Added value} : (1 + Sp)$$
$$Sp = Ua + Ba + Oa$$
$$P = ((Fc * PC) + Vc + Pg) * (1 + Sp)$$

where Fc is the Fixed costs, Vc the Variable costs, Pg the Profit goal or profit margin, Sp the Service premium, Ua the Unit-level activity, Ba the Batch-level activity, and Oa is the Other activity.

It is important to note that the ABC method is still subjective, because the cost determination for the service offering is done by the seller. The advantage of this approach is that the different service elements are evaluated by their costs and not by the suspected value for the customer. The total value for the customer is therefore what they receive and not what they desire or expect. Consequently, it is easier to put a monetary label on the service component.

The ABC analysis provides a structure that compares each service activity with resources it consumes (Lovelock and Wirtz, 2004). As mentioned before, this is an important consideration in a customer-oriented pricing model. Our framework enables the management to enhance customer relationships by embedding services in the price equation.

5.4. Fourth step: Comparing the price to the market price

The present research identified several factors that influence the price setting process. One important aspect that has so far not been considered is competitors' actions. Our respondents identified this factor as very important. Therefore, the calculated price is compared to average competitors' prices and adjustments are made accordingly.

Summing up, the present proposed pricing framework allows the company to determine the resources needed for each market segment, thus resulting in more precise price estimates. Moreover, the present customer-specific method enables the management to focus on relationship-building, which in turn should have a positive impact on the company's bottom line.

6.   Limitations and Recommendations for Future Research

This chapter has several limitations. First, the present findings are limited to the specific research context. Companies in other industries might provide very different results. Second, it can be argued that maximisation of sales, profits, market share, etc. might be unrealistic (Boone and Kurtz, 2002; Keil *et al.*, 2001; Kotler, 1997). For example, lack of communication easily hinders maximisation as a goal. Moreover, the present research identified a lack of structure in the coordination of the responsibility for the service offerings. These loose structures signal inefficient communication within the company. Third, the calculation of the service premium is somewhat limited as it does not necessarily represent the buyer's perception of value (Forbis and Mehta, 1981). Finally, decision-making under uncertainty was not taken into account in our framework. Competitive moves, which are often difficult to predict, represent a certain risk in the decision-making process. If a company serves different geographical areas, the amount of uncertainty increases, thus further complicating the price setting process (Forman and Hunt, 2004). Price-setting under uncertainty is a fruitful area for future research.

References

Anderson, J and J Narus (1999). *Business Market Management*. Sydney: Prentice Hall.

Avlonitis, GJ and KA Indounas (2005). Pricing objectives and pricing methods in the services sector. *Journal of Services Marketing*, 19(1), 47–57.

Boone, LE and DL Kurtz (2002). *Contemporary Marketing*, 10th Ed. Cincinatti, OH: Thomson Learning, Southwestern.

Cox, JL (2001). Can differential prices be fair? *Journal of Product & Brand Management*, 10(5), 264–275.

Diamantopoulus, A (1991). Pricing: Theory and evidence — A literature review. In *Perspectives on Marketing Management*, MJ Baker (ed.). London: Wiley.

Diamantopoulus, A and B Mathews (1995). *Making Pricing Decisions: A Study of Managerial Practice*. London: Chapman & Hall.

Eugster, CC, JN Kakkar and EV Roegner (2000). Bringing discipline to pricing. *The McKinsey Quarterly*, 14(1), 132–139.

Forbis, JL and NT Mehta (1981). Value-based strategies for industrial products. *Business Horizons*, 24 (May–June), pp. 32–42.

Forman, H and JM Hunt (2004). Managing the influence of internal and external determinants on international industrial pricing strategies. *Industrial Marketing Management*, 34, 133–146.

Forsyth, JE, A Gupta, S Haldar and MV Marn (2000). Shedding the commodity mind-set. *The McKinsey Quarterly*. Available from http://www. mckinseyquarterly.com/article_page.aspx?ar=950&L2=3&L3=41.

Gijsbrechts, E and K Campo (2000). Pricing. In *The Oxford Textbook of Marketing*, K Blois (ed.). New York, NY: Oxford University Press.

Gummesson, E (2004). Qualitative research in marketing — Road-map for a wilderness of complexity and unpredictability. *European Journal of Marketing*, 39(3/4), 309–327.

Hinterhuber, A (2004). Towards value-based pricing — An integrative framework for decision making. *Industrial Marketing Management*, 33, 765–778.

Hoffmann, KD, LW Turley and SW Kelley (2002). Pricing retail services. *Journal of Business Research*, 55, 1015–1023.

Hoffmann, KD and DR Arnold (1989). Professional service pricing: An extended cost-oriented approach. *Journal of Professional Services Marketing*, 5(1), 29–39.

Keil, SK, D Reibstein and DR Wittink (2001). The impact of business objectives and the time horizon of performance evaluation on pricing behaviour. *International Journal of Marketing Research in Marketing*, 18, 67–81.

Kothandaraman, P and DT Wilson (2001). The future of competition: Value-creating networks. *Industrial Marketing Management*, 30(4), 379–389.

Kotler, P (1997). *Marketing Management: Analysis, Planning, Implementation and Control*, 9th Ed. Upper Saddle River, NJ: Prentice-Hall.

Kotler, P, G Armstrong, J Saunders and V Wong (1999). *Principles of Marketing*, 2nd Ed. Upper Saddle River, NJ: Prentice Hall Europe.

Lancioni, R (2005). Pricing issues in industrial marketing. *Industrial Marketing Management*, 34, 111–114.

Lancioni, R, HJ Schau and MF Smith (2005). Intraorganizational influences on business-to-business pricing strategies: A political economy perspective. *Industrial Marketing Management*, 34, 123–131.

Lere, JC (2000). Activity-based costing: A powerful tool for pricing. *Journal of Business & Industrial Marketing*, 15(1), 23–33.

Lovelock, C and J Wirtz (2004). *Services Marketing — People, Technology, Strategy*. Upper Saddle River, NJ: Prentice Hall.

Marsh, G (2000). International pricing — A market perspective. *Marketing Intelligence & Planning*, 18(4), 200–205.

McCarthy, EJ and WD Perrault (1993). *Basic Marketing: A Managerial Approach*, 11th Ed. Homewood, IL: Irwin.

Myers, MB (1997). The pricing of export products: Why aren't managers satisfied with the results? *Journal of World Business*, 32(3), 277–289.

Myers, MB, ST Cavusgil and A Diamantopoulous (2002). Antecedents and actions of export pricing strategy — A conceptual framework and research proposition. *European Journal of Marketing*, 36(1/2), 159–188.

Oxenfeldt, AR (1983). Pricing decisions: How they are made and how they are influenced. *Management Review*, November, pp. 23–25.

Qu, R and CT Ennew (2003). An examination of the consequences of market-orientation in China. *Journal of Strategic Marketing*, September, 201–214.

Reichheld, FF and EW Sasser (1998). Zero-Migration: Dienstleister im Sog der Qualitätsrevolution [Zero-Migration: Service provider in the suction of the quality revolution]. In *Handbuch Kundenbindungsmanagement*, M Bruhn and C Homburg (eds.), pp. 135–150. Wiesbaden: Gabler Verlag (in German).

Samiee, S (1987). Pricing in marketing strategies of US and foreign based companies. *Journal of Business Research*, 15(March), 17–30.

Samiee, S and K Roth (1992). The influence of global marketing standardization on performance. *Journal of Marketing*, 56(April), 1–17.

Sawhney, M and PM Kotler (2001). Marketing in the age of information democracy. In *Kellogg on Marketing*, D Lacobucci (ed.), pp. 386–409. New York, NY: Wiley.

Shimp, AT (2003). *Advertising, Promotion, & Supplemental Aspects of Integrated Marketing Communications*. Mason, OH: Thompson, Southwestern.

Simon, H (1989). *Price Management*. Amsterdam: North-Holland.

Smith, GE (1995). Managerial pricing orientation: The process of making pricing decisions. *Pricing Strategy & Practice*, 3(3), 28–39.

Sotgui, F and F Ancarani (2004). Exploiting the opportunities of internet and multi-channel pricing. *Journal of Product & Brand Management*, 13(2), 125–136.

Thompson, KN and BJ Coe (1997). Gaining sustainable competitive advantage through strategic pricing: Selecting a perceived value price. *Pricing Strategy & Practice*, 5(2), 70–79.

Tung, W, LM Capella and PK Tat (1997). Service pricing: A multi step synthetic approach. *The Journal of Services Marketing*, 11(1), 53–65.

Yin, RK (1994). *Case Study Research*, 2nd Ed. Thousand Oaks, CA: Sage Publications.

Yip, GS (1989). Global strategy in a world of nations? *Sloan Management Review*, 31, Fall, 29–41.

Zeithaml, VA, PR Varadarajan and CP Zeithaml (1988). The contingency approach: Its foundations and relevance to theory building and research in marketing. *European Journal of Marketing*, 22(7), 37–64.

RESEARCH METHODOLOGY PAPERS

8

TESTING SIGNIFICANCE OF VARIABLES IN REGRESSION ANALYSIS WHEN THERE IS NON-NORMALITY OR HETEROSKEDASTICITY. THE WILD BOOTSTRAP AND THE GENERALISED LAMBDA DISTRIBUTION

E. Pavlidis, I. Paya and D. A. Peel

University of Lancaster Management School, UK

Statistical inference on the parameters of regression models requires special precautions when the error term is heteroskedastic and/or non-normal. In this case, although conventional test statistics do not follow t and F distributions, simulation methods can be used to draw inferences. We discuss two methods: the wild bootstrap and the generalised lambda distribution. By employing both artificial and real-world data from the National Footbal League, we show that these methods may prove particularly useful in hypothesis testing.

Keywords: Heteroskedastic; non-normality; Monte Carlo simulations; wild bootstrap; generalised lambda distribution.

1. Introduction

The significance of the variables in the linear model is tested

$$y_t = X_t \beta + \varepsilon_t, \tag{1}$$

where y_t is a dependent variable, X_t is an exogenous vector of explanatory variables and β is the unknown parameter.

It is assumed that y and X are stationary variables,[1] that the error term is independent[2] of previous errors, so that:

$$E\varepsilon_t\varepsilon_{t-j} = 0 \quad \text{for } j = 1 \text{ to } \infty.$$

If the error term in Eq (1) is normally distributed and has constant variance then the method of least squares and t or F-statistics are employed to test the significance of the explanatory variables, X. Inference on the parameter, β, requires alternative methods to be employed when the error terms are either non-normal or heteroskedastic.[3] When the errors are non-normal, the standard errors of the least squares estimators may exhibit bias.[4] When the error term is heteroskedastic, so that the variance of the error term is not constant, the OLS estimator of the covariances of the estimates of β are in general biased and inconsistent. As a consequence conventional significance tests are not distributed as t and F distributions. Mispecification of a true model, which does not exhibit non-normal or heteroskedastic errors, could results in non-normal or heteroscedasticity errors in the estimated, and incorrect, functional form. It is assumed that this is not the rationale for empirical finding of non-normality or heteroskedasticity.

Although the White (1980) method permits asymptotically correct inferences in the presence of heteroskedasticity of unknown form, it is known that in finite samples, t- and F-tests can be seriously biased (see e.g., MacKinnon and White, 1985; Chesher and Jewitt, 1987).

Therefore, the question arises here as to how to make appropriate statistical inferences. Two methods are discussed,[5] both exploit recent advances in computing.

The first of these is known as the wild bootstrap (see, e.g., Wu, 1986; Mammen, 1993; Davidson and Flachaire, 2001). The method can be employed when the sample size is small. This method is appropriate when the error term in a regression exhibits heteroskedasticity and the error is

---

[1] Otherwise we have issues related to non-stationary variables (see, e.g., Hendry, 1995).
[2] Bootstrap methods that are appropriate for serially correlated errors are discussed in Politis (2003).
[3] A variety of tests available for testing non-normality or heteroskedasticity. See e.g., Eviews package.
[4] See, e.g., Dasgupta and Mishra (2004).
[5] Other methods for handling non-normality exist. One well-known method is to employ the LAD or MAD estimator (see e.g., Dasgupta and Mishra, 2004).

either normally or non-normally distributed. Under such conditions the wild bootstrap has been shown to be an appropriate method for determining the appropriate critical values for t- and F-tests and also it can be appropriate when the error is non-normal and there may be no statistical evidence of heteroskedasticity (see Gonçalves and Kilian, 2004).

The second method is only appropriate when the error term exhibits non-normality. The method involves simulating errors from the generalised lambda distribution (GLD) that can match the first four moments of the empirical moments of the error distribution. The intuition behind both the wild bootstrap approach and the generalised lambda approach is to identify the distributions of relevant test statistics when the null hypothesis holds and the distribution of regression residuals is based on the relevant sample distribution.

Both methods with reference to the simple equation are illustrated:

$$y_t = \alpha + \beta x_t + \varepsilon_t, \tag{2}$$

where interest lies in testing whether $\hat{\alpha} = 0; \hat{\beta} = 1$.

1.1. The wild bootstrap

Eq (2) is estimated by ordinary least squares. The vector of residuals from this regression is denoted as $\hat{\varepsilon}$.

A new series of pseudo-residuals based on $\hat{\varepsilon}$ are created:

$$\varepsilon_{i0} = \hat{\varepsilon} e_i, \tag{3}$$

$$\varepsilon_{j0} = \hat{\varepsilon} \omega_i, \tag{3a}$$

where e_i and ω_i are drawn from one of the following two-point distributions:

$$e_i = \begin{cases} -(\sqrt{5} - 1)/2 & \text{with probability } \dfrac{(\sqrt{5} + 1)}{(2\sqrt{5})}, \\ (\sqrt{5} + 1)/2 & \text{with probability } 1 - \dfrac{(\sqrt{5} + 1)}{(2 + 5)}, \end{cases} \tag{4}$$

or

$$\omega_i = \begin{cases} 1 & \text{with probability } 0.5, \\ -1 & \text{with probability } 0.5. \end{cases} \tag{5}$$

Both e_i and ω_i are mutually independent drawings from a distribution independent of the original error distribution. The error distribution has the first four moments:

$$Ee = 0, \quad Ee^2 = \sigma_e^2 = 1, \quad Ee^3 = s_e = 1, \quad Ee^4 = k_e = 2,$$

$$E\omega = 0, \quad E\omega^2 = \sigma_\omega^2 = 1, \quad E\omega^3 = s_\omega = 0, \quad E\omega^4 = k_\omega = 1,$$

where σ^2 = variance, s = skew and k = kurtosis.

Because the errors are independent, the first four moments of the new and composite errors (3) and (3a) are given by:

$$E\varepsilon_{i0} = E\hat{\varepsilon}e_i = 0, \quad \sigma_{i0}^2 = \sigma_{\hat{\varepsilon}}^2.1, \quad s_{i0} = s_e 1, \quad k_{i0} = k_{\hat{\varepsilon}}2,$$

$$E\varepsilon_{j0} = E\hat{\varepsilon}\omega_i = 0, \quad \sigma_{j0}^2 = \sigma_{\hat{\varepsilon}}^2.1, \quad s_{j0} = 0, \quad k_{j0} = k_{\hat{\varepsilon}}1.$$

As a consequence the errors exhibit the same variance structure as the original regression residuals, so that the heteroskedasticity in the pseudo-residuals matches with the regression residuals. However, we note that the two-point distributions mismatch kurtosis and skewness, respectively. More specifically, the distribution in Eq (3) matches any skewness inherent in the original regression residuals and overstates the kurtosis by a factor of 2; the distribution in Eq (3a), on the other hand preserves the kurtosis in the distribution of the original residuals, though it eliminates any skewness in the original distribution.

The empirical procedure is to create a large number of times (e.g., 9999) simulated (or artificial) series for y, denoted by y^i, where the null hypothesis $\hat{\alpha} = 0$, $\hat{\beta} = 1$ is imposed employing the actual values of x but using the pseudo-residual series. Therefore:

$$y^i = x + \varepsilon_{i0} = \hat{\varepsilon}e_i \quad \text{for } i = 1 \text{ to } 9999.$$

In turn, y^i, $i = 1$ to 9999 is regressed on x and the estimated intercept and slope coefficients are saved.

It is known that the generated sequences of simulated data have a true intercept of 0 and true slope of unity *by construction*. However, the estimated parameter values will, in general, differ from the true values. From the 9999 iterations, there is an empirical distribution for $\hat{\alpha} = 0$, $\hat{\beta} = 1$ together with their associated standard errors. This distribution is based solely on re-sampling the residuals of the original regression. From this distribution appropriate critical values of test statistics such as the t- and F-statistic consistent without rejecting the null hypothesis at an appropriate level of significance (e.g., 5%) can be obtained. These critical values can then be employed to determine whether the estimates obtained from Eq (2) employing real data are consistent with rejection of the null.

A variant of the wild bootstrap is to employ a similar procedure that might be more robust to "abnormal" or outlier observations in the explanatory variables (see Cribari-Neto and Zarkos, 1997).[6]

Of course, it can be the case that inferences made on least squares standard errors are the same as those made employing the standard errors from least squares regression. However, least squares inference is inappropriate theoretically and you would not know if it makes a difference in inference unless alternative methods are employed.

To illustrate the possible differences this can make, a dataset with 100 observations is simulated by the following scheme:

The explanatory variable, X, follows a gamma distribution with parameters $(1,1)$, [Eviews@rgamma $(1,1)$], v is drawn from a t distribution with degrees of freedom [Eviews@rtdist (5)], and j is created from a uniform distribution — lying between -1 and 1 as Eviews@runif $(-1,1)$. Now, the error is created as $u = v * (1 + j)^{0.5}$. Finally Y was created as $Y = X + 2 * u$. This procedure ensures that the error exhibits both heteroskedasticity and possible non-normality. The least squares regression gave:

$$Y_t = 0.4 + 0.65X_t + \varepsilon_t$$
$$(0.30)\ (0.23).$$
$$\bar{R}^2 = 0.067.$$

Jarque–Bera p value $= 0.055$.
White test for heteroskedasticity $= 0.01$.

Least squares t values in parenthesis.

It is noted that there is only marginal evidence of non-normality in the regression residuals on the basis of the Jarque–Bera test but significant hetroskedasticity on the basis of the White test.

The critical values at the 5% level obtained from the wild bootstraps were respectively, -2.42 and 2.44 for the $1, -1$ version and -2.16 and 2.02 for the other version. Consequently, on this basis, the coefficient on X as unity cannot be rejected. [t stat from regression $= (1 - 0.65)/0.23$ which lies within the bounds].[7]

---

[6] They proposed an alternative bootstrap method that take into the effect into account influential or outlier observations. Code for this version in Eviews format is available from the authors.

[7] For comparison 2.5% 97.5% the critical values from the t-distribution and the normal bootsrap are t-distr -1.984217 1.984217, t-slope.normal boot -2.007154 1.921918.

The code in Eviews for the two wild bootstraps is given in Appendix A.

1.2. *The generalised lambda distribution*

The GLD is a flexible tool for modelling and simulating random variables. Its attractiveness lies in the fact that it can assume a wide variety of shapes. To this end, it can accurately approximate many commonly used statistical distributions,[8] as well as describe the real world data for which the distribution form is not known. Moreover, because its percentile or inverse distribution defines it, functions like Monte Carlo simulations are implemented with relative ease (see Karian and Dudewizc (2000) for a thorough analysis). Applications of the GLD include modelling of personal income data (Tarsitano, 2004), option pricing when prices are not log-normally distributed (Corrado, 2001), and the evaluation of tests concerning distributional forecast when forecast errors deviate from normality (Noceti *et al.*, 2003).

1.2.1. *Definition and properties*

Ramberg and Schmeiser (1974) proposed the following percentile function as an extension of Tukey's one parameter lambda distribution:

$$F^{-1}(u) = \lambda_1 + \frac{u^{\lambda_3} - (1 - u)^{\lambda_4}}{\lambda_2}, \qquad (6)$$

for u in $[0, 1]$. The corresponding probability density function expressed in terms of percentiles is:

$$f(x) = f(F^{-1}(u)) = \frac{\lambda_2}{\lambda_3 u^{\lambda_3 - 1} - \lambda_4 (1 - u)^{\lambda_4 - 1}}.$$

Parameters λ_1 and λ_2 are the location and scale parameters, respectively, while λ_3 and λ_4 determine the skewness and the kurtosis. The latter two parameters also determine whether the support of the GLD is finite, half-infinite or infinite by controlling the tails of the density function. It should be noted that not all the combinations of the parameter values result in valid

---

[8]For example, the normal, the log-normal and the gamma distributions. Moreover, by choice of the parameters one can create distributions with desired values of skewness and kurtosis. Parameter values that generate particular values of skewness and kurtosis are tabulated in Karian and Dudewicz [2000]. This makes it a valuable tool as a generator of distributions with particular characteristics in simulation.

statistical distributions. Due to the fact that $f(x)$ must be non-negative and integrate to unity; there are regions of the parameter space in which the GLD is not well-defined. These are described in Karian and Dudewizc (2000) and King and MacGillivray (1999).

1.2.2. *Fitting the GLD*

Empirical applications require the estimation of the parameter values of the GLD. Several competing methods have been suggested in the literature for fitting the GLD to the data (see Su, 2007). In this study, we adopt the method of moments (MM) of Ramberg *et al.* (1979) and the starship method (ST) developed by King and MacGillivray (1999). The former approach consists of equating the first four sample moments to expressions for the GLD moments and using a minimisation procedure, such as Newton's, to solve the parameter values (Karian and Dudewizc, 2000). However, different parameter values may give rise to the same moments implying that the GLD may in fact provide a poor fit to the data. This is illustrated in Fig. 1, which shows four GLDs with different parameters but with the same four moments.

Unlikely, the method of moments the starship directly addresses this issue. It consists of three stages:

(1) Specify a range of the lambda parameters and apply a reverse transformation to the data.
(2) Calculate the value of a goodness of fit measure, such as the Anderson–Darling or the Kolmogorov–Smirnov, for the closeness of the resulting series to the uniform (0, 1).
(3) Select the set of parameters with the best goodness of fit.

The main drawback of the starship is that it can be extremely slow for large samples.

1.2.3. *Empirical methodology*

Of course, because the application of the GLD requires homoskedastic residuals, the question arises; why not use the standard bootstrap of Efron (1979) where samples are drawn at random with replacement. This bootstrap should be employed and is reported for comparison in some applications below. However, the bootstrap method can only draw new samples from the sample data points. Fitting a GLD to the data points means that data samples will

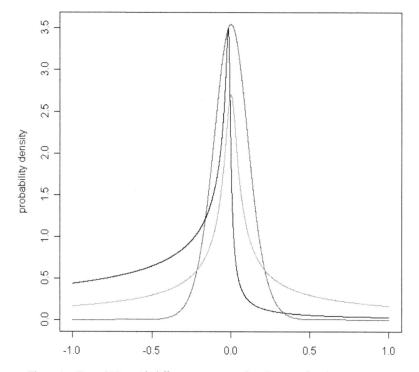

Figure 1.   Four GLDs with different parameters but the same first four moments.

be drawn from the whole fitted distribution and not solely the data points in the sample. Karian and Dudewicz (2000) suggest that this method can do better than the normal bootstrap when the sample is small and as well as when it is large. There seems to be some unresolved questions. Namely, the implications of fitting the "wrong distribution" to the sample data points. However, the GLD is an interesting addition to the inferential tool kit.

To illustrate, two datasets have been used. First, artificial data, while, for the second the data from the National Football League is employed. As in the previous sections the underlying regression equation is Eq (2) and the null hypothesis is $\alpha = 0$, $\beta = 1$. However, in this case the fact that the error term is not characterised by heteroskedasticity motivates us to generate pseudo-series for the dependent variable by employing the GLD. In particular, we estimate Eq (2) and we obtain the estimated residual series $\hat{\varepsilon}$. Since the distribution of e is assumed to be unknown, even for the artificial example, two GLDs to $\hat{\varepsilon}$ are fitted by employing the MM and ST methods. The

GLD-ST is the distribution that provides the best fit to the data according to the Anderson–Darling measure, while the GLD-MM has the same first four sample moments with the estimated residuals. Having specified the parameters of the two GLDs we create 9999 series of pseudo-residuals by drawing values from the uniform $(0, 1)$ and calculating Eq (6). The standard bootstrap and the wild bootstrap are used for comparison reasons. In turn, the null is imposed and the dependent variable is calculated as the sum of the explanatory and the pseudo-residuals.

1.2.4. *Artificial example*

An explanatory variable X and an error term are created by drawing 500 values from the Gamma$(1, 1)$ and $t(5)$, respectively. The dependent variable y is set equal to their sum. Next, we run regression Eq (2) to obtain the estimated coefficients and the residuals, $\hat{\varepsilon}$.

The kurtosis and skewness of $\hat{\varepsilon}$ are 10.65 and -1.03, respectively, while the Jarque–Bera normality test[9] rejects the null hypothesis for all conventional significance levels. The deviation from normality is also clear from Fig. 2, which shows the histogram of $\hat{\varepsilon}$ along with the probability density functions of the two fitted GLDs and of a normal distribution fitted by maximum likelihood. The regression results and the critical t values based on the t-distribution with 499 degrees of freedom, the GLD-MM, the GLD-ST, the bootstrap and the wild Bootstrap are presented in Table 1. While the F-statistic and the critical values for the aforementioned methods are shown in Table 2.

Although hypotheses $\hat{a} = 0$ and $\hat{B} = 1$ cannot be rejected in all cases, there are significant differences between the alternative methods. In contrast to the confidence interval for the t-distribution, all other confidence intervals are asymmetric. For example, the t critical values for the intercept according to the GLD-ST are -1.647 and 2.234, while for the t-distribution they are ± 1.965. Generally, the GLD-MM and the bootstrap methods provide values close to the t-distribution, implying that the effect of non-normality is not severe. On the other hand, the confidence intervals for the wild bootstrap are much wider, which suggests that larger t-statistics are needed to reject the null hypotheses.

For the F-statistic, reported in Table 2, the critical values for all methods are higher than the ones of the F-distribution with the difference increasing as

---

[9]JB $= 1681.139$, p value $= 0$.

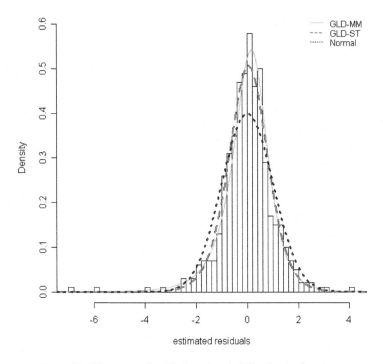

Figure 2.   Histogram of residuals and probability density functions.

Table 1.   Regression results and critical t values.

	$\hat{a}$		$\ddot{B}-1$	
Estimate	−0.059		0.05	
t-statistic	−0.969		1.18	
	$t_{0.025}$	$t_{0.975}$	$t_{0.025}$	$t_{0.975}$
t-distribution	−1.965	1.965	−1.965	1.965
GLD-MM	−1.951	2.043	−2.030	1.937
GLD-ST	−1.647	2.234	−1.911	1.993
Bootstrap	−1.856	2.028	−2.006	1.903
Wild bootstrap	−2.407	2.345	−2.855	2.950

we move from 5% significance level to 1%. The GLD-MM and the bootstrap provide again almost the same critical values, which are slightly higher than the ones of the F-distribution and slightly smaller than the ones of GLD-ST. On the contrary, the wild bootstrap suggests much larger critical values than the other methods.

Table 2. Critical values of F-statistic.

F-statistic	0.715	
	$F_{0.95}$	$F_{0.99}$
F-distribution	3.014	4.648
GLD-MM	3.059	4.845
GLD-ST	3.295	5.051
Bootstrap	3.061	4.759
Wild bootstrap	5.034	7.182

1.2.5. Statistical efficiency of the National Football League betting market

Efficiency of the spread bet in the National Football League remains the subject of an ongoing debate. For instance, Russo *et al.* (1989) do not reject efficiency contrary to Cain *et al.* (2000). An important issue in this context is the fact that the variables under examination are non-normal.[10]

Standard tests of statistical efficiency are based on the regression equation

$$\text{DIFF} = a + b\text{SPREAD} + \varepsilon, \qquad (7)$$

where DIFF denotes the difference between the actual points scored by the home and the away teams, and SPREAD is the bookmakers' prediction of the points difference. For the market to be efficient, the coefficients a and b should be equal to 0 and 1, respectively. Typically, the above equation is estimated by least squares and t and F tests are used in order to test the null. However, Reep and Benjamin (1968) suggest that the points scoring process in sports follow the negative binomial distribution. Since the difference of two negative binomial distributions is not normal, hypothesis tests based on the aforementioned procedure will be suspect (Cain *et al.*, 2000), which motivates the use of simulation techniques.

Regression statistics of Eq (7) employing 1966 observations and simulation results are presented in Tables 3 and 4.

Overall, $\hat{a}$ and $\hat{b}$ are not statistically different from 0 and 1 at the 5% significance level, suggesting that statistical efficiency in the National Football League betting market cannot be rejected. Further, the critical values reported in Rows 6–9 of Table 3 are very close to those of the t-distribution with two

---

[10]There is also the issue of heteroskedasticity. However, White's test did not detect the presence of heteroskedacity for the examined data set ($F = 0.931$, $p = 0.394$).

Table 3.   Regression results for NFL and critical t values.

	$\hat{a}$		$\hat{b}-1$	
Estimate	0.419		−0.046	
t-statistic	1.236		−0.923	
	$t_{0.025}$	$t_{0.975}$	$t_{0.025}$	$t_{0.975}$
t-distribution	−1.961	1.961	−1.961	1.961
GLD-MM	−1.968	1.944	−1.945	1.984
GLD-ST	−1.766	2.137	−1.936	1.989
Bootstrap	−1.996	1.979	−1.934	2.003
Wild bootstrap	−1.936	1.948	−1.904	1.883

Table 4.   Regression results for NFL and critical F values.

	0.859	
F-statistic	$F_{0.95}$	$F_{0.99}$
F-distribution	3.000	4.616
GLD-MM	3.011	4.583
GLD-ST	3.083	4.877
Bootstrap	3.086	4.860
Wild bootstrap	2.873	4.385

exceptions. The GLD-ST resulted in asymmetric confidence intervals for the intercept and the wild bootstrap in smaller critical values. The critical values of the wild bootstrap are also smaller for the F-statistic. On the contrary, the GLD-MM critical values are similar to those of the F-distribution, while for GLD-ST and the bootstrap are slightly larger.

A possible explanation for these findings is that non-normality is not as severe as in the previous example. The kurtosis and skewness of the residuals are 3.238 and 0.029, while the Jarque-Bera test[11] rejects the null hypothesis only at the 5% significance level.

2.   Conclusions

We have discussed two methods that might prove useful statistical inference in models that exhibit either non-normality or heteroskedasticity. The code is provided in Appendix A.

---

[11] The JB statistic is 7.088 and the p value is 0.029.

Appendix A. Simulation Code

A.1. *Bootstrap*

```
!n=10000
create u 1 !n

vector(!n) ac1
vector(!n) ac2
vector(!n) atc1
vector(!n) atc2
vector(!n) ase2
vector(!n) atestb
vector(!n) awald

!sa=100
smpl 1 !sa

series z=@rgamma(1,1)

series t=@rtdist(5)
series t=(t-@mean(t))/@stdev(t)

series s2=1+@runif(-1,1)

series e=t*(@sqrt(s2))

series y=z+e

param c(11) 0 c(12) 0
equation equ.ls y=c(11)+c(12)*z
equ.makeresids u
stom(u,umat)

for !i=1 to !n

smpl 1 !sa
vector(!sa) rres!i
rres!i=@resample(umat)
```

```
mtos(rres!i,rress!i)
series yb!i=z+rress!i
smpl 1 100
param c(1) 0 c(2) 1 c(3) 0 c(4) 0
equation equ{!i}.ls yb!i=c(1)+c(2)*z
ac1(!i)=equ{!i}.@coefs(1)
ac2(!i)=equ{!i}.@coefs(2)
atc1(!i)=equ{!i}.@tstats(1)
atc2(!i)=equ{!i}.@tstats(2)
ase2(!i)=equ{!i}.@stderrs(2)
atestb(!i)=(ac2(!i)-1)/ase2(!i)
freeze(tab!i) equ{!i}.wald c(1)=0,c(2)=1
awald(!i)=@val(tab!i(7,2))
'awaldp(!i)=@val(tab!i(7,4))
delete eq* yb* re* rr* k* tab*

next

smpl 1 !n

mtos(ac1,c1)
mtos(ac2,c2)
mtos(atc1,t1)
mtos(atc2,t2)
mtos(atestb,tb)
mtos(awald,wald)
scalar cl=@quantile(t1,0.025)
scalar cu=@quantile(t1,0.975)
scalar bl=@quantile(tb,0.025)
scalar bu=@quantile(tb,0.975)
scalar w=@quantile(awald,0.95)

delete a*
delete c1 c2 e s2 t* u* wald y z

pagestruct(freq=u, start=1, end=!n)
```

A.2. Wild bootstrap

```
!n=10000
create u 1 !n
vector(!n) ac1
vector(!n) ac2
vector(!n) atc1
vector(!n) atc2
vector(!n) ase2
vector(!n) atestb
vector(!n) awald

!sa=100
smpl 1 !sa

series z=@rgamma(1,1)

series t=@rtdist(5)
series t=(t-@mean(t))/@stdev(t)

series s2=1+@runif(-1,1)

series e=t*(@sqrt(s2))

series y=z+e

param c(11) 0 c(12) 0
equation equ.ls y=c(11)+c(12)*z
equ.makeresids u
stom(u,umat)

for !i=1 to !n
series k!i=@rbinom(1,0.72361)
stom(k!i,kmat!i)

for !g=1 to !sa

vector(!sa) rres!i
```

```
if kmat!i(!g)>0 then
                rres!i(!g)=umat(!g)*(-0.618034)
                mtos(rres!i, rress!i)
else
                rres!i(!g)=umat(!g)*1.618034
                mtos(rres!i,rress!i)
endif
next

smpl 1 !sa
series yb!i=z+rress!i

smpl 1 100
param c(1) 0 c(2) 1 c(3) 0 c(4) 0
equation equ{!i}.ls yb!i=c(1)+c(2)*z
ac1(!i)=equ{!i}.@coefs(1)
ac2(!i)=equ{!i}.@coefs(2)
atc1(!i)=equ{!i}.@tstats(1)
atc2(!i)=equ{!i}.@tstats(2)
ase2(!i)=equ{!i}.@stderrs(2)
atestb(!i)=(ac2(!i)-1)/ase2(!i)
freeze(tab!i) equ{!i}.wald c(1)=0,c(2)=1
awald(!i)=@val(tab!i(7,2))
'awaldp(!i)=@val(tab!i(7,4))

delete eq* yb* re* rr* k* tab*

next

smpl 1 !n

mtos(ac1,c1)
mtos(ac2,c2)
mtos(atc1,t1)
mtos(atc2,t2)
mtos(atestb,tb)
mtos(awald,wald)
scalar cl=@quantile(t1,0.025)
scalar cu=@quantile(t1,0.975)
```

```
scalar bl=@quantile(tb,0.025)
scalar bu=@quantile(tb,0.975)
scalar w=@quantile(awald,0.95)
delete a*
delete c1 c2 e s2 t* u* wald y z

pagestruct(freq=u, start=1, end=!n)
```

A.3. *Generalised lambda distribution*

```
' Note: the reported statistic is the Chi-Square
!n=200
create u 1 !n

vector(!n) ac1
vector(!n) ac2
vector(!n) atc1
vector(!n) atc2
vector(!n) ase2
vector(!n) atestb
vector(!n) awald


' The vector of lambdas is determined by the Method of Moments
in Maple using the program of Karian and Dudewicz(2000),
' or by using the starship method of King and MacGillivray
(1999) in Rproject.

scalar lambda1=-0.2937
scalar lambda2=-0.3658
scalar lambda3=-0.1047
scalar lambda4=-0.1833

!sa=100
smpl 1 !sa

series z=@rgamma(1,1)

series t=@rtdist(5)
series t=(t-@mean(t))/@stdev(t)
```

```
' s2 is set equal to 1, which implies no heteroskedasticity
series s2=1
series e=t*(@sqrt(s2))

series y=z+e

param c(11) 0 c(12) 0
equation equ.ls y=c(11)+c(12)*z
equ.makeresids u
stom(u,umat)

for !i=1 to !n

smpl 1 !sa
series gld!i=@runif(0,1)
series rress!i=lambda1+(gld!i^lambda3-(1-gld!i)^
lambda4)/lambda2
series yb!i=z+rress!i

smpl 1 100
param c(1) 0 c(2) 1 c(3) 0 c(4) 0
equation equ{!i}.ls yb!i=c(1)+c(2)*z
ac1(!i)=equ{!i}.@coefs(1)
ac2(!i)=equ{!i}.@coefs(2)
atc1(!i)=equ{!i}.@tstats(1)
atc2(!i)=equ{!i}.@tstats(2)
ase2(!i)=equ{!i}.@stderrs(2)
atestb(!i)=(ac2(!i)-1)/ase2(!i)
freeze(tab!i) equ{!i}.wald c(1)=0,c(2)=1
awald(!i)=@val(tab!i(7,2))
'awaldp(!i)=@val(tab!i(7,4))

delete eq* yb* re* rr* k* tab* gld*

next

smpl 1 !n
```

```
mtos(ac1,c1)
mtos(ac2,c2)
mtos(atc1,t1)
mtos(atc2,t2)
mtos(atestb,tb)
mtos(awald,wald)
scalar cl=@quantile(t1,0.025)
scalar cu=@quantile(t1,0.975)
scalar bl=@quantile(tb,0.025)
scalar bu=@quantile(tb,0.975)
scalar w=@quantile(awald,0.95)


delete a*
delete c1 c2 e s2 t* u* wald y z lambda*


pagestruct(freq=u, start=1, end=!n)
```

A.4.   Bootstrap, wild bootstrap and GLD in R-project

```
############################################################
#      Hypotheses Testing with Non Normal Residuals      #
############################################################
# Statistical Software: R project,
# Required Packages: car, MASS, gld, moments

m <- 1000;              # number of replication;

n <- N <- 500;          # sample size
x <- rgamma(N,1,1);     # the explanatory variable follows
                          a gamma (1,1) distribution
tr <- rt(500,4);        # the error term follows a t(4)
                          distribution
tr <- tr/sd(tr);        # the error term standardized
y <- x+tr;              # calculating the dependent
                          variable


lr <- lm(y~x);          # the regression
s.lr <- summary(lm(y~x)); # the summary of the regression
res <- s.lr$residuals;  # the estimated residuals
```

```
## Testing the Hypothesis that the intercept and the slope
equal 0 and 1
lh <- lht(lr,c("(Intercept)=0","x=1"));
# The Generalized Lambda Distribution

# The first vector of lambdas is determined by the method of
moments in
# Maple using the program of Karian of Dudewicz, 2000.
ll <- c(0, 1, 0.14, 0.14);

# The starship method for determnining lambdas of King and
#MacGillivray(1999)
st <- starship(res,param="rs",initgrid=list(lcvect=c(-.06,
 -.04,0,.05,.1,.15, .2,.3,.5),ldvect=c(-.3,-.2,-.15,-.03,
0,.05,.1,.15,.2,.3,.5)));
# The second vector of Lambdas
sll <- st$lambda;

# Plotting the Histogram of the residuals and the probability
densities
hist(res,breaks=25,freq=FALSE);
plotgld(ll,param="rs",new.plot=FALSE,col=3);
plotgld(sll,param="rs",new.plot=FALSE,col=2);

#Comparison with the normal distribution

an <- fitdistr(res,"normal"); # fitting the normal
distribution
curve(dnorm(x,an[[1]][1],an[[1]][2]),col=4,add=T); # plotting
the normal distribution

# The vectors of F statistics for the GLD-MM, GLD-ST, the
Bootstrap
# and the Wild Bootstrap:
f.1 <- f.2 <- f.3 <- f.4 <- f.5 <- vector();

# The vectors of t statistics for the GLD-MM, GLD-ST, the
Bootstrap
```

```
# and the Wild Bootstrap:
t1.inter <- t2.inter <- t3.inter <- t4.inter <- t5.inter
<- vector();
t1.slope <- t2.slope <- t3.slope <- t4.slope <- t5.slope
<- vector();


# Generation of Pseudo Series according to the null hypothesis
# and new critical values

for(i in 1:m){
    y.f1 <- x+rgl(n,ll,param="rs");        # GLD-MM
    y.f2 <- x+rgl(n,sll,param="rs");       # GLD-ST
    y.f3 <- x+sample(res,n,replace=T);     # Bootstrap
    y.f4 <- x+res*sample(c(-1,1),n,replace=T); #Wild Bootstrap
    reg.f1 <- lm(y.f1~x);
    reg.f2 <- lm(y.f2~x);
    reg.f3 <- lm(y.f3~x);
    reg.f4 <- lm(y.f4~x);
    s.reg.f1 <- summary(reg.f1);
    s.reg.f2 <- summary(reg.f2);
    s.reg.f3 <- summary(reg.f3);
    s.reg.f4 <- summary(reg.f4);

    f.1[i] <- lht(reg.f1,c("(Intercept)=0","x=1"))$F[2];
    f.2[i] <- lht(reg.f2,c("(Intercept)=0","x=1"))$F[2];
    f.3[i] <- lht(reg.f3,c("(Intercept)=0","x=1"))$F[2];
    f.4[i] <- lht(reg.f4,c("(Intercept)=0","x=1"))$F[2];

    t1.inter[i] <- s.reg.f1$coef[1,3];
    t2.inter[i] <- s.reg.f2$coef[1,3];
    t3.inter[i] <- s.reg.f3$coef[1,3];
    t4.inter[i] <- s.reg.f4$coef[1,3];

    t1.slope[i] <- (s.reg.f1$coef[2,1]-1)/s.reg.f1$coef[2,2];
    t2.slope[i] <- (s.reg.f2$coef[2,1]-1)/s.reg.f2$coef[2,2];
    t3.slope[i] <- (s.reg.f3$coef[2,1]-1)/s.reg.f3$coef[2,2];;
    t4.slope[i] <- (s.reg.f4$coef[2,1]-1)/s.reg.f4$coef[2,2];
}
```

```
# Critical Values for the F.test
F.gld.mm <- quantile(f.1,c(0.95,0.99));
F.gld.star <- quantile(f.2,c(0.95,0.99));
F.boot <- quantile(f.3,c(0.95,0.99));
F.wboot <- quantile(f.4,c(0.95,0.99));


F.distr <- vector();
sl <- c(0.95,0.99);
for(i in 1:2){
      F.distr[i] <- qf(sl[i],df1=2,df2=N-2); # 2 restrictions,
      2 parameters
}


summary.f <- rbind(F.distr,F.gld.mm,F.gld.star,F.boot,F.wboot);
colnames(summary.f) <- c("95%","99%");


# Critical Values for the t test (intercept)

t.inter.gld.mm <- quantile(t1.inter,c(0.025,0.975));
t.inter.gld.star <- quantile(t2.inter,c(0.025,0.975));
t.inter.boot <- quantile(t3.inter,c(0.025,0.975));
t.inter.wboot <- quantile(t4.inter,c(0.025,0.975));


t.distr <- vector();
sl <- c(0.025,0.975);
for(i in 1:2){
      t.distr[i] <- qt(sl[i],df=N-1);
}


summary.t.inter <- rbind(t.distr,t.inter.gld.mm,t.inter.gld
        .star, t.inter.boot,t.inter.wboot);
colnames(summary.t.inter) <- c("2.5%","97.5%");


# Critical Values for the t test (slope)
t.slope.gld.mm <- quantile(t1.slope,c(0.025,0.975));
t.slope.gld.star <- quantile(t2.slope,c(0.025,0.975));
t.slope.boot <- quantile(t3.slope,c(0.025,0.975));
t.slope.wboot <- quantile(t4.slope,c(0.025,0.975));
```

```
t.distr <- vector();
sl <- c(0.025,0.975);
for(i in 1:2){
    t.distr[i] <- qt(sl[i],df=N-1);
}


summary.t.slope <- rbind(t.distr,t.slope.gld.mm,t.slope.gld
.star, t.slope.boot,t.slope.wboot);
colnames(summary.t.slope) <- c("2.5%","97.5%");


###### Results
s.lr;                  # regression results
lh;
# Descriptive Statistics for the Residuals
dstats.resid <-
round(c(mean(res),median(res),var(res),skewness(res),
kurtosis(res)),3);
names(dstats.resid ) <- c("mean","median","variance",
"skew","kurtosis")
dstats.resid;


summary.t.inter;
summary.t.slope;
summary.f;
```

References

Cain, M, D Law and DA Peel (2000). Testing for statistical and market efficiency when forecast errors are non-normal: The NFL betting market revisited. *Journal of Forecasting*, 19, 575–586.

Chesher, A and I Jewitt (1987). The bias of a heteroskedasticity consistent covariance matrix estimator. *Econometrica*, 55, 1217–1222.

Cribari-Neto, F and SG Zarkos (1999). Bootstrap methods for heteroskedastic regression models: Evidence an estimation and testing. *Econometric Reviews*, 18, 211–228.

Corrado, CJ (2001). Option pricing based on the generalized lambda distribution. *Journal of Future Markets*, 21, 213–236.

Dasgupta, M and SK Mishra (2004). Least absolute deviation estimation of linear econometric models: A literature review. Mimeo North-Eastern Hill University, Shillong.

Davidson, R and E Flachaire (2001). The wild bootstrap, tamed at last. Working Paper, Department of Economics, Queen's University, Kingston, Ontario.

Efron, B (1979). Bootstrap methods: Another look at the jackknife. *Annals of Statistics*, 7, 1–26.

Gonçalves, S and L Kilian (2004). Bootstrapping autoregressions with conditional heteroskedasticity of unknown form. *Journal of Econometrics*, 123, 89–120.

Hendry, DF (1995). *Dynamic Econometrics*. Oxford: Oxford University Press.

Karian, Z and E Dudewicz (2000). *Fitting Statistical Distributions: The Generalized Lambda Distribution and Generalized Bootstrap Method*. Boca Raton, FL: CRC Press.

King, R and H McGillivray (1999). A starship estimation method for the generalized Lambda distributions. *Australia and New Zealand Journal of Statistics*, 41(3), 353–374.

MacKinnon, JG and H White (1985). Some heteroskedasticity consistent covariance matrix estimators with improved finite sample properties. *Journal of Econometrics*, 29, 305–325.

Noceti, P, J Smith and S Hodges (2003). An evaluation of tests of distributional forecasts. *Journal of Forecasting*, 22, 447–455.

Politis, DN (2003). The impact of bootstrap methods on time series analysis. *Statistical Science*, 18, 219–230.

Ramberg, J and B Schmeiser (1974). An approximate method for generating asymmetric random variables. *Communications of the Association for Computing Machinery*, 17, 78–82.

Ramberg, J, P Tadikamalla, E Dudewicz and E Mykytka (1979). A probability distribution and its uses in fitting the data. *Technometrics*, 21, 201–214.

Reep, C and B Benjamin (1968). Skill and chance in association football. *Journal of the Royal Statistical Society, Series A*, 131, 581–585.

Russo, B, J Gandar and R Zuber (1989). Market rationality tests based on cross-equation restrictions. *Journal of Monetary Economics*, 24, 455–470.

Su, S (2007). Numerical maximum log likelihood estimation for generalized lambda distributions. *Computational Statistics and Data Analysis*, 51(8), 3983–3998.

Tarsitano, A (2004). Fitting the generalized lambda distribution to income data. In *Compstat 2004 — Proceedings of the International Conference on Computational Statistics*, pp. 815–822. Heidelberg, Germany: Physica-Verlag.

White, H (1980). A heteroskedasticity-consistent covariance matrix estimator and a direct test for heteroskedasticity. *Econometrica*, 48, 817–838.

Wu, CFJ (1986). Jackknife, bootstrap and other re-sampling methods in regression analysis (with discussion). *Annals of Statistics*, 14, 1261–1295.

9

METHOD OF DNA COMPUTING
AND ITS APPLICATION TO
GROUP MANAGEMENT

Junzo Watada

Waseda University, Japan

The objective of this chapter is to illustrate the method of DNA computing and based on this understanding, to explain the application to group controlling of elevators.

Many non-deterministic polynomial time (NP) complete problems are solved using heuristic and approximate methods instead of providing a complete solution or mathematical optimal approaches. The central reason comes from the huge computation time needed to solve such combinatorial problems by means of a conventional silicon computer based on von Neumann's architecture. To solve such NP complete problems, this chapter provides an alternative and innovative method based on nano size of DNA to obtain infinitively in a life such as silicon. This chapter is an introductory explanation.

The group management is treated as an example of its application. Inefficient situations have been encountered such that all elevators are moving in the same direction or that all elevators arrive at the same floor even during rush hours in the morning. To resolve such situations all elevators should be controlled to assign the best elevator to passengers according to time-to-time change of passengers. The group control system is employed in selection of driving patterns according to the change of traffic volumes or driving management in accidents. Such a group control realises comfortable, safe, and economical management of elevators. The objective of this chapter is to apply DNA computing to calculate complex and huge combinatorial problems of a group of elevators and huge number of floors. The optimal solution will be presented to the group control of elevators on the basis of the DNA computing.

Keywords: DNA computing; optimise scheduling algorithm; group management system.

1. Introduction

The objective of this paper is to illustrate the method of DNA computing and based on this understanding, to explain the application to group controlling of elevators.

Many NP complete problems are solved using heuristic and approximate methods instead of providing a complete solution or mathematical optimal approaches. The central reason comes from the huge computation time to solve such combinatorial problems by means of a conventional silicon computer based on von Neumann's architecture. To solve such NP complete problems, this paper provides an alternative and innovative method based on nano size of DNA to obtain infinitively in a life such as silicon. This paper is an introductory explanation.

The group management is treated as an example of its application. Theoretical studies of applied DNA computing research (Adleman, 1994; Kim *et al.*, 2006) are spare. Especially, optimise scheduling algorithm problems (Adleman, 1998; Amos *et al.*, 2002; Ito and Fukusaki, 2004; van Noort, 2004) have been intensively studied. Genetic algorithm is a kind of soft computing with genetic mechanism in organisms and searches optimal values when it assumes a number of control patterns in repeating general algorith (GA) simulation. Therefore, development group management systems have been intensively studied for improvement of an elevator's transportation efficiency and convenience. The usage condition and operation pattern that manages the elevator hourly are changed as a gene through generations. The GA obtains the economical passenger's satisfaction rating.

In GA, computing mimics an organism's evolution process. Thus, for searches it needs fast processing and huge computer materials. On the other hand, in DNA computing, because the computing mimics DNA copy mechanism in chemical reaction, it processes massive parallels which can overcome the GA problem.

It is usual that multiple elevators are provided in a high building. Effective control of elevators is important in the high building. The elevator group controlling system has to effectively control elevators so that it makes all passengers feel satisfied and provides the most efficient use of the elevator system. The problem is to decide which elevator should stop at a floor where a passenger is waiting.

Recently, artificial intelligence has been employed to the controlling of elevators. On the other hand, inefficient situations have been encountered during rush hours in the morning such that all elevators are moving in the same direction or that all elevators arrive on the same floor. To resolve such situations all elevators should be controlled to be best assigned to passengers according to time-to-time change of passengers. The group control system is employed in selection of driving patterns according to the random change of traffic volumes or driving management. Such a group control realises comfortable, safe, and economical management of elevators.

2. DNA Computing

A DNA computer is wet computation, which is based on the high ability of special molecule recognition executed in the reaction among DNA molecules. Leonard M. Adleman reported the molecule computation in science (Adleman, 1994). He found that a DNA polymerase, which has an enzyme function of copying a DNA, is very similar to the function of a Turing machine. The DNA polymerase composes its complementary DNA molecule using a single strand helix of a DNA molecule as a mould. On the basis of this characteristic, if the huge amount of DNA molecules are mixed in a test tube, the reaction among the DNA molecules is in parallel pursued at the same time. Therefore, when a DNA molecule can express data or program and the reaction among DNA molecules is executed, it is possible to realise super-parallel processing and a huge volume of memories in comparison with a present conventional electronic computer.

For example, it is common in a molecular biological experiment to deal with 6×10^{16}/ml of DNA molecules. So this means to realise 60,000 Tbytes of memories, if one string of a DNA molecule expresses one character. The total executing speed of a DNA computer can outshine a conventional electronic computer even if the execution time of one DNA molecule reaction is relatively slower than the conventional computer. DNA computing is appropriate for tackling such a problem as analysis of Genome information and functional designing of a molecule which have molecules as input data.

Since Adleman showed the method to solve a directed Hamiltonian path problem with seven cities using DNA molecules (Adleman, 1994), research have been pursued on a theoretical study to realise general computation on the basis of DNA molecules. R.J. Lipton's solution of hard computational problems is one step towards such research. Adleman has developed a computing model to realise, by an experimental treatment on DNA molecules, operations on multiple sets of characters strings after coding finite alphabet characters using DNA molecules.

3.   Method of DNA Computing

The main idea behind DNA computing is to adopt a wet biological technique as an efficient computing vehicle where data are represented using a DNA strand itself. Even though a DNA reaction is slower than a silicon-based machine, the inherent parallel processing offered by the DNA process plays an important role. This parallelism of the DNA processing is of particular interest to NP problems.

Since then, the DNA computation has been a challenging technique to solve NP problems in various fields and applications. Real DNA capabilities are explored beyond the limitation of silicon machines. DNA computing has been applied to various fields such as nanotechnology, scheduling (Jeng *et al.*, 2007; Watada *et al.*, 2006), combinatorial optimisation (Ouyang *et al.*, 1997), boolean circuit development (Owenson *et al.*, 2001), and so on.

As mentioned above, DNA molecules are used as information storage media. Usually, DNA sequences of about 8–20 base-pairs are used to represent bits, and numerous methods have been developed to manipulate and evaluate them. To manipulate a wet technology into a computational approach, several techniques such as ligation, hybridisation, polymerase chain reaction (PCR), gel electrophoresis, and enzyme reaction are used as computational operators for copying, sorting, and splitting or concatenating information in DNA molecules. The next subsection will describe briefly the biochemical process adopted in the DNA computing technique.

3.1.   *Encoding scheme*

In the DNA computational procedure, a main process is to encode each of the objects of a focal problem into a DNA sequence. In this process, the data have been encoded into DNA sequences regarding the design. The correct design is essential in order to get the optimal result. A wrong design will result in a wrong sequence after the ligation process.

3.2.   *Ligation and hybridisation*

When DNA sequences are spoided in a test tube using a dropper as shown in Fig. 1, the DNA sequences recombine with each other in the test tube by means of some enzyme reaction as shown in Fig. 1. This process is called

Figure 1. Droppers for spoiding and hybridising.

ligation. All the DNA sequences used in the experiment with some complement will be mixed together into one test tube. Normally, the oligonucleotide or DNA mixture is heated to 95°C and cooled to 20°C at 1°C/min for hybridisation as shown in Fig. 1. The reaction was then subjected to a ligation. At the end of the process, a certain DNA sequence will ligate together with another DNA sequence so as to produce a new sequence.

3.3. *Polymerase chain reaction (PCR)*

PCR is a process that quickly amplifies the amount of specific molecules of DNA in a given solution using primer extension by polymerase. DNA polymerases perform several functions, including the repair and duplication of DNA. Each cycle of the reaction doubles the quantity of this molecule, giving an exponential growth in the number of sequences.

3.4. *Affinity separation*

The objective of an affinity separation process is to verify whether all the data have some strands. This process permits single strands containing a given subsequence v to be filtered out from a heterogeneous pool of other sequences. After synthesising strands complementary to v and attaching them to magnetic beads, the heterogeneous solution is passed over the beads. Those strands containing v anneal to the complementary sequence and are retained. Strands not containing v pass through without being retained.

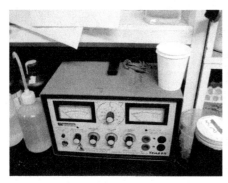

Figure 2.   Electrophoresis.

Normally, in this process, a double-stranded DNA is incubated with the Watson–Crick complement of data that is conjugated to magnetic beads. Only single-stranded DNA molecules are retained that the sequences of data are annealed to the bound. So, the process is repeated.

3.5. Gel electrophoresis

Gel electrophoresis is an important technique for sorting DNA strands by their size (Amos *et al.*, 2002). Electrophoresis enables charged molecules to move in an electric field as shown in Fig. 2. Basically, DNA molecules carry negative charge. So that, when kept in an electrical field, they tend to migrate towards a positive pole. Since DNA molecules have the same charge per unit length, they all migrate with the same force in an electrophoresis process. Smaller molecules, therefore, migrate faster through the gel, and thus they can be sorted according to their size. Usually, agarose gel is used as a medium in this process. At the end, the resulted DNA is taken in a picture as shown in Fig. 3.

4. Comparison with Program

However, a DNA computing technique employs completely different tactics when they allocate an independent letter code such as ATCG, GTAC, or CAAC, to each of samples. Next, DNA sequences corresponded to a number of possible combinations would be prepared. After they are hybridised in super parallel, the remaining DNA fragments are amplified to obtain

Figure 3. Camera.

an answer sequence and the procedure is carried out only once (Ito and Fukusaki, 2004).

DNA computation creates all different feasible solutions at once. It is the main benefit of using DNA computation in solving complex problems. This is known as parallel processing. Humans and most electronic computers must solve the problem step by step, known as linear processing. DNA itself provides the added benefits of being a cheap, energy-efficient resource (Adleman, 1998).

(1) Separate (T, s): The operation separates given set T into set, $+(T, s)$, of characters including character string s and set, $-(T, s)$ of character strings without character string s. This operation corresponds to abstract experiment on DNA molecules in a test tube.

(2) Mix: The operation mixes sets T_1 and T_2 into union set $T_1 \cup T_2$. This operation corresponds to mixed test tubes T_1 and T_2.

(3) Detect (T): Detect (T) returns YES if T is not empty and NO if T is empty in a test tube. The operation corresponds to the experimental treatment

that detects the existence of DNA molecules by electrophoretical fluorescent method.

(4) Amplify (T): The operation corresponds to create multi-sets T_1 and T_2 with the same contents as given set T. This is amplifying the experimental treatment that amplifies the amount of molecules using PCR.

This treatment corresponds to experimental treatment to amplify the amount of molecules.

The most important nature of a DNA molecule is the Watson and Crick complimentarity to realise a DNA computing.

DNA consists of four bases of molecule structures named as adenine A, guanine G, cytosine C, and thymine T, which has a connecting rule of DNA such as A can connect only with T and G can connect only with C. This connecting rule is called the Watson–Crick complementarity. This nature is essential to realise the above-mentioned separate operation. That is, it is possible to separate a partial string of characters "ad" so that a DNA sequence complementary to the DNA denoting "ad" is marked, input into a test tube, hybridised to form a double-strand helix of DNA and abstracted. And also this nature enables to create randomly a set of character strings according some rule.

In the Adleman's model a set of character strings is computed according to a program denoted using four kinds of instructions mentioned above. Using this computation an NP complete problem can be solved by algorithm based on production-detection method PCR. The DNA computer is a computing method to solve real-world problems using this nature.

5. Group Management System

Suppose that a building has n floors and m elevators, Fig. 4 shows the position of each elevator, the destination of passengers in each elevator and the direction of passengers on each floor.

As Table 1 shows, the input information is as follows:

(1) Present position of elevator $1 - m$
(2) Destination floors indicated in an elevator
(3) Summoning an elevator from a floor

Based on the information, the problem is to manage elevators as efficiently as possible.

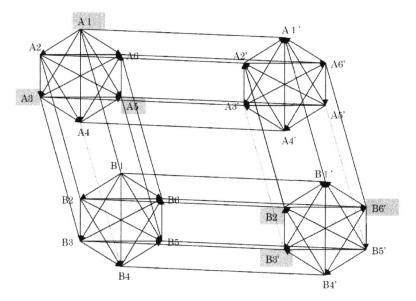

Figure 4.   Whole paths of two elevators.

Table 1.   Managing information of elevators.

Floor	Queuing	Elevator(1)	Elevator(2)	$\cdots$	Elevator(m)
N	↓				
$N-1$	↓		$(1, 3, 5)$		
⋮					
3					$(4, N-1, N)$
2		$(3, 4, N-1)$			
1	↑				

Notation. The problem is deciding on the optimal diagram of m elevators with shortest total waiting time of a queue when the waiting queue and the initial position of each elevator is at time t:

i : Floor number where a present elevator is
j : Next destination floor of the elevator
T_E : Staying time of an elevator at each floor
$T(i, j)$: Moving time of an elevator from floor i to floor j

Using the abovementioned notations, we have the following:

$$T(i, j) = T(j, i) = f(|j - i|) \tag{1}$$

Therefore, we can write the moving time $T(i,j)$ of the elevator from floor i to floor j can be expressed by the function $f(|j - i|)$ of the deference between j and i. This function decides the weight of an edge from node i to node j.

That is:

$$\psi_1 = f(1) + T_E(1)$$
$$\psi_2 = f(2) + T_E(2)$$
$$\vdots$$
$$\psi_9 = f(9) + T_E$$

Therefore, denoting $|j - i| = k$, then:

$$\psi_k = f(k) + T_E \qquad (2)$$

where $1 \leq k \leq N - 1$.

The movement of an elevator has been illustrated using a graph. The elevator at floor 1 has $N-1$ possible passes for destination floor $j (2 \leq j \leq N)$; movement time can be calculated as:

$$\psi_k = f(k) + T_E \quad (1 \leq k \leq N - 1) \qquad (3)$$

whole movements are shown as in Fig. 5. Each weight on the edge is denoted in Fig. 5.

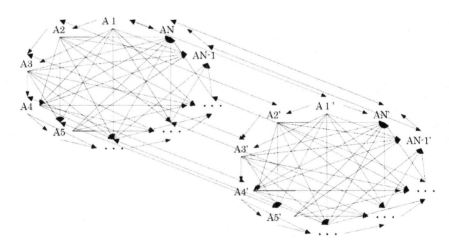

Figure 5.   Whole movements of Elevator A.

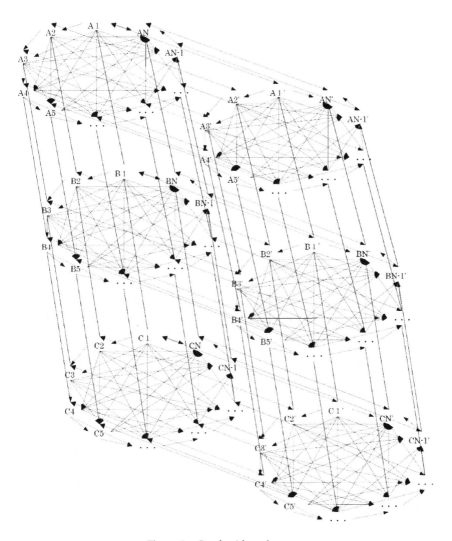

Figure 6.   Graph with m elevators.

As there are m elevators, which can duplicate m graphs shown in Fig. 6 and connecting between all vertexes as in one graph shown in Fig. 7.

Therefore, it is sufficient that one of m elevators may reach the calling floor on the line of graph $A, B, \ldots, m$. A graph has been writted on each of the cases where Elevator A or Elevator B, elevator m reach the floor, when the button is pushed on a floor. Considering all combinatorial, the shortest

Floor	Calling	Elevator A	Elevator B
6			(2,3)
5	↓		
4	↑		
3	↓		
2			
1		(3,5)	

Figure 7.   Managing information of elevators.

pass of each graph $A, B, \ldots, m$ has been calculated. The largest value out of graphs $A, B, \ldots, m$ has been denoted by $f(A, B, \ldots, m)$.

By calculating all combinatorial $f_x(A, B, \ldots, m)$; The optimal allocation of elevators can be obtained by selecting the minimum value of $f_x(A, B, \ldots, m)$. x denotes the number of combinatorial. For example, when the number of elevators is 2 and the summons from floors is 3, the number of combinatorial is 2^3.

It is possible to illustrate Elevator B by a graph as in the case of Elevator A. Figure 4 illustrates the graph of all paths of two Elevators A and B.

Floor 4 is downward-summoned at Floors 2 and 3. One of Elevators A or B stops for these summons. That is, the optimal management of the elevators is to schedule efficiently elevators.

Now, Elevator A is at Floor 1 and its destination floors are 3 and 5. The destination floors of Elevator B are 2 and 3. There are upward summons. Figure 4 shows the floors with a coloured mark where each elevator should stop.

In this case, if the destination floor is decided for one of Elevators A and B, then the other elevator is automatically assigned to the destined floor. As a result, it is necessary to calculate the optimal paths for two kinds of graphs of Elevators A and B. The larger value for both Elevators A and B is denoted by $f_x(A, B)$.

At the end the problem here is to select the smallest value $\min[f_x(A, B), (x = 1, \ldots, 8)]$. The obtained schedule which gives the smallest value is the optimal solution for Elevators A and B. There are 16 kinds of graphs that can be obtained from eight combinatorial shown in Fig. 8. Section 6 shows how to calculate the shortest path schedule for both elevators.

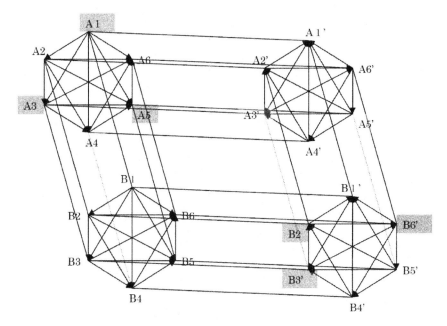

Figure 8.   Behaviour example of Elevators *A* and *B*.

6. DNA Approach to Optimal Solution of a Group Management of Elevators

In DNA computation, each base sequence is assigned to each floor as shown in Table 2.

The connection between two bases sequences corresponding to each floor has been denoted as the movement between two floors (the black in Fig. 9 of movement root).

Table 2.   Correspondence between floor and bases sequence.

1	2	3	4	5	6
AAAA	*CCCC*	*TTTT*	*ATAT*	*GAGA*	*GGGG*
1′	2′	3′	4′	5′	6′
CACA	*TcTC*	*TGTG*	*GCGC*	*CAGT*	*GATC*

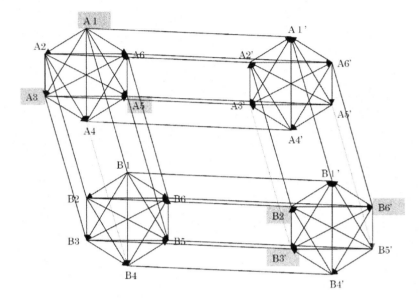

Figure 9.   Movement 5 of Elevators *A* and *B*.

An appropriate length of DNA sequences has been assigned to the edge weight.

$$rll\psi_k = f(k) + T_E$$

$\psi_1 = f(1) + T_E$ string of two random characters(ZZ)

$$\vdots$$

$\psi_5 = f(5) + T_E$ string of ten random characters$(YYYYYYYYYYYYYYYYYYYY)$

$$f(A, B) = \max\,(4 + 4 + 4 + 4 + 4, 4 + 2 + 4 + 4 + 4 + 2 + 4 + 4 + 4 + 4)$$

$$= \max\{20, 36\} = 36$$

These values show the spending time for the movement between two floors, which are combined in the base sequence. In this problem all movements between floors are 40 roots. DNA sequences corresponding to these roots which denote red portion in Table 3 are produced.

DNA fragments corresponding to a floor in Table 2 and red portions of DNA fragments corresponding to a root in Table 3 are produced. Then, put these DNA fragments and combining polymerase in the same test tube

Table 3.   Representation of roots by DNA sequence (edge DNA oligonucleotides).

1 → 2	AAZZCC TTEEGG	6′ → 5′	GAZZGT CTEECA
1 → 3	AAWWWWTT TTFFFFAA	6′ → 4′	GAWWWWCG CTFFFFGC
1 → 4	AAVVVVVVAT TTHHHHHHTA	6′ → 3′	GAVVVVVVTG CTHHHHHHAG
1 → 5	AAXXXXXXXXGA TTIIIIIIIICT	6′ → 2′	GAXXXXXXXXTC CTIIIIIIIIAG
1 → 6	AAYYYYYYYYYYGG TTJJJJJJJJJJCC	6′ → 1′	GAYYYYYYYYYYCA CTJJJJJJJJJJGT
2 → 2′	CCTC GGAG	5′ → 5	CAZZGA GTEECT
2 → 3	CCZZTT GGEEAA	5′ → 4′	CAZZCG GTEEGC
2 → 4	CCWWWWAT GGFFFFTA	5′ → 3′	CAWWWWTG GTFFFFAC
2 → 5	CCVVVVVVGA GGHHHHHHCT	5′ → 2′	CAVVVVVVTC GTHHHHHHAG
2 → 6	CCXXXXXXXXGG GGIIIIIIIICC	5′ → 1′	CAXXXXXXXXCA GTIIIIIIIIGT
3 → 3′	TTTG AAAC	4′ → 4	GCAT CGTA
3 → 4	TTZZAT AAEETA	4′ → 3′	GCZZTG CGEEAC
3 → 5	TTWWWWGA AAFFFFCT	4′ → 2′	GCWWWWTC CGFFFFAG
3 → 6	TTVVVVVVGG AAHHHHHHCC	4′ → 1′	GCVVVVVVCA CGHHHHHHGT
4 → 4′	ATCG TAGC	3′ → 3	TGTT ACAA
4 → 5	ATZZGA TAEECT	3′ → 2′	TGZZTC ACEEAG
4 → 6	ATWWWWGG TAFFFFCC	3′ → 1′	TGWWWWCA ACFFFFGT
5 → 5′	GACA CTGT	2′ → 2	TGCC CTGG
5 → 6	ATZZGG TAEECC	2′ → 1′	TGZZCA CTEEGT
6 → 6′	GGGA CCCT	1′ → 1	CAAA GTTT

and stare the test tube at appropriate temperature, and all combinatorial are automatically created.

Various DNA sequences are automatically created by combining fragments shown as each floor in Table 2 and filaments shown as each movement root in Table 3. These DNA sequences are corresponding to combinatorials

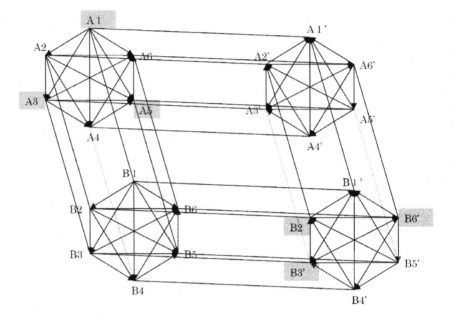

Figure 10.   Movement 1 of Elevators A and B.

of feasible solutions. To solve the graph shown in Fig. 10, DNA sequences which have "*AA*" (the former two characters upward at the first floor) at the start and "*GA*" (the latter two characters upwards at the fifth floor) at the end are detected, out of many DNA sequences, using various polymerase.

As the floors where elevators should stop are known, only DNA sequences with $AA * TTTT* GA$ are selected that the DNA sequences are starting from "*AA*" and pass through "*TTTT*" and terminated at "*GA*". Then, the shortest DNA sequence shows the optimal solution to start from the 1st floor, stop at the 3rd floor and reach the 6th floor. This procedure can be abstracted by the weight of a DNA sequence. It is because a long DNA sequence is heavy and a short DNA sequence is light. At the end the DNA sequence has been checked and changed it to a floor number.

The shortest roots for the graphs are obtained from the following DNA sequences and the length of these DNA sequences can be calculated. The shortest sequence is the schedule that Elevator A stops at the 4th floor and Elevator B stops at the 3rd and 5th floors. Therefore, the optimal schedule for Elevators A and B is obtained for the present state of elevators and calling floors. If this computation is pursued to obtain the optimal schedule whenever buttons are pushed at a calling floor, the schedule with the shortest waiting time can be obtained.

7. Conclusions

"It is not the world that attracts attention now and that a usual physical law sways in the minute (nano) world but the world of a quantum-mechanics-law". This is described in the famous uncertainty principle which Heisenberg in Germany discovered in 1927. Although a present computer is built on the model of a deterministic Turing machine, a new idea of a quantum Turing machine has not been built into a model yet. The computer based on this idea is called a quantum computer, and the idea is required to go further beyond the present computer. Although this type of computer does not yet exist in the real world, a present computer (von Neumann type computer) using the semiconductor should faith the wall of combinatorial problems.

There are also many problems including the following:

— Reparation and extraction requires too much time.
— Error happens in copying DNA

Although there are problems which must be solved to realise a DNA computer, it is expected that modern technology will replace the present von Neumann-type computer. In the future work, hall calling occur randomly with version space method learning.

References

Adleman, L (1994). Molecular computation of solutions to combinatorial problems. *Science*, 266, 1021–1024.

Adleman, LM (1998). Computing with DNA. *Scientific American*, 54–61.

Amos, M, G Paun, G Rozenberg and A Salomaa (2002). Topics in the theory of DNA computing. *Journal of Theoretical Computer Science*, 287, 3–38.

Ito, Y and E Fukusaki (2004). DNA as a "Nanomaterial". *Journal of Molecular Catalysis B: Enzymatic*, 28, 155–166.

Jeng, DJ-F, J Watada and I Kim (2007). Solving a real time scheduling problem based on DNA computing. *Soft Computing Journal* (in press).

Kim, I, DJ-F Jeng and J Watada (2006). Redesigning subgroups in a personnel network based on DNA computing. *International Journal of Innovative Computing, Information and Control*, 2(4), 885–896.

van Noort, D (2004). Towards a re-programmable DNA computer. Berlin Heidelberg: Springer-Verlag. DNA9, LNCS 2943, pp. 190–196.

Ouyang, Q, PD Kaplan, S Liu and A Libchaber (1997). DNA solution of the maximal clique problem. *Science*, 278, 446–449.

Owenson GG, M Amos, DA Hodgson and A Gibbsons (2001). DNA-based logic. *Soft Computing*, 5(2), 102–105.

Heorghe PG, G Rozenberg and A Salomaa (1999). *DNA Computing: New Computing Paradigms*. Translated Edition by T Yokomori. Springer (in Japanese).

Rohani BAB, J Watada and W Pedrycz (2006). A DNA computing approach to data clustering based on mutual distance order. In *Proceedings of the 9th Czech-Japan Seminar*, 18–22 August 2006, Kitakyusyu and Nagasaki, pp. 139–145.

Watada J, S Kojima, S Ueda and O Ono (2006). DNA computing approrch to optimal decision problem. *International Journal of Innovative Computing, Information and Control*, 2(1), 273–282.

Winfree E, F Lin, LA Wenzler and NC Seeman (1998). Design and self-assembly of two-dimensional DNA crystals. *Nature*, 394(6693), 539–549.

INDEX